blues
and the poetic
spirit

by paul garon

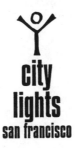

**city
lights**
san francisco

First published by Eddison Press, Ltd., London, 1975

Cover photo: Amy van Singel
Cover design: Rex Ray
Book design: Elaine Katzenberger
Typography: Harvest Graphics

Library of Congress Cataloging-in-Publication Data:

Garon, Paul
    Blues and the poetic spirit / Paul Garon. — Rev. and
expanded ed.
        p.   cm.
    Includes bibliographical references.
    ISBN 0-87286-315-8
    1. Blues (Music) — History and criticism. I. Title.
    ML3521.G37   1996   96-936
    782.421643'09 — dc20   CIP
                                                      MN

CITY LIGHTS BOOKS are edited by Lawrence Ferlinghetti and
Nancy J. Peters and published at the City Lights Bookstore,
261 Columbus Avenue, San Francisco, CA 94133.

ACKNOWLEDGMENTS

MY SPECIAL THANKS TO FRANKLIN ROSEMONT FOR SUPPLYING quotations from French texts and to James C. Anderson who provided inestimable aid in photographic research. Valuable photographic assistance was also provided by Amy van Singel and Diane Allmen. Without the technical assistance of Margaret O'Connor, Tony Russell, Penny Martin, and Franklin Rosemont, this book could not have taken its present form.

This new edition has profited from discussions with Beth Garon, Michael Boggs, Jim O'Neal, Pen Bogert, Brenda Bogert, Burnham Ware, and the members of Blues-l.

Grateful acknowledgment is made to the photographers, copyright holders and owners listed below for permission to reproduce the photographs used in this book:

Diane Allmen
Jean-Jacques Jack Dauben
Paul Garon
Living Blues (Amy van Singel)
                    (Jim O'Neal)
Phillip Manti
Ronald L. Papp
University of Louisville Photographic Archives

* * *

The reader should note that inaudible and indecipherable lyrics are indicated by parentheses, and that further, where the first line of a verse is repeated, the designation (x2) follows the first line rather than a transcription of the second line.

contents

introduction

WHEN *BLUES AND THE POETIC SPIRIT* WAS PUBLISHED IN 1975, the blues seemed to be coming to the end of its long history. Yet, now, in 1996, the blues is still going strong. Indeed, from several perspectives it is stronger than ever. I would like to take this opportunity, then, to emphasize just a few of those aspects of the blues that are most dynamic and alive, those aspects that continue to forge a path for the spirit of liberation, and that guarantee us the revelation of poetry in our lives, if we are only willing to follow them. Some are old currents still alive, while others are newly found relationships, forged in the strain of the cultural clashes and developments of the 1990s, but they all contribute to the vitality of the blues today.

The powerful tradition of generations succeeding generations is nothing new in the blues or in any of the arts. In one of the most moving passages in Mike Rowe's 1977 interview with Billy Boy Arnold, Arnold describes how excited he was — in the 1950s — to be walking down the street "with the great Big Bill [Broonzy]." By the time of the interview, long after his hit *I Wish You Would,* Arnold himself was one of the greats, and it is always affecting to see one of your heroes engaging in hero worship! Today, he is back on the scene with several new CDs on the market, and one can easily imagine the young harp players of the '90s ecstatic over the possibility of walking down the street "with the great Billy Boy Arnold." Indeed, many "living legends" appear so frequently in blues clubs and festivals that the same venue often hosts stars like Otis Rush, Buddy Guy, Koko Taylor, Jimmy Rogers, James Wheeler or Ruth Brown, along with "newer" performers like Lonnie Pitchford, Rosie Ledet, Sugar Blue, Deborah Coleman, Chicago Bob Nelson or Shirley King.

It's significant that so many women performers are on this list. In the vaudeville era, the blues' most famous performers were women like Ma Rainey, Mamie Smith and Bessie Smith, but as vaudeville ended, many of these stunning artists found themselves without work. At the end of their lives, their death certificates often read "home maker" instead of "singer" or "musician." Some did become jazz and cabaret artists, but others languished; a few, like Alberta Hunter and Sippie Wallace, staged successful comebacks in the 1970s and 1980s.

The social and economic forces that worked to diminish the role of women in the blues throughout several decades are weakening in the 1980s and 1990s. (They had already weakened in the post-World War II years that saw the rise of R & B.) More and more female blues artists appear at clubs and festivals, and women are again reclaiming their rightful place in the blues spotlight. These women bring to the blues their own gendered performance styles that establish patterns of eroticism and tension that — like male performance — become a nexus for feminist critique and understanding. For while the blues operates under its own dialectic of freedom and repression, it illuminates the nature of our limitations just as it provides a glimpse of the potential for our liberation. For this reason, it can easily function to articulate women's desires, just as it equally articulates the male demand for love and affection, and the longings of humanity in general.

There are other specific examples of the blues' "universal" appeal that are especially compelling in the 1990s: Gay and lesbian listeners and performers identify strongly with lesbian artists like Gladys Bentley and songs like Ma Rainey's *Prove It On Me Blues* and George Hannah's *Freakish Man Blues.* And just as sufferers from diverse afflictions in the 1920s identified with the protagonists of songs like *TB Blues* and *Meningitis Blues,* so listeners today who have illnesses like TB, AIDS, and cancer may respond to the same performances.

One particular aspect of the blues spectrum is undergoing unusual popularity and growth: zydeco music. This black French music derived from Cajun, Afro-American and Afro-Caribbean traditions began to absorb R & B and blues influences in the early 1950s, thanks to Clarence Garlow, Boozoo Chavis, and most significantly Clifton Chenier. Today it often reaches out to newer sounds while trying simultaneously to maintain its roots in the Louisiana/Texas soil, but its appeal to the blues audience is signal, and it continues to be one of the most popular of blues-influenced music styles.

Blues has always been a music of jook joints and clubs — not to mention the back porch, the house, or the picnic ground — and clubs still supply the most credible venue for blues performance. Most inspiring is the fact that countless jook joints of Mississippi still host local bands every weekend. While the performers are rarely "name" acts, they are often the young and eager aspirants who are keeping the blues alive on its native turf. Clubs like the Blue Front in Bentonia, Thompson's Grocery in Bobo, and Junior Kimbrough's in Holly Springs keep the Mississippi flame burning brightly.

These artists and their clubs are important signs of the blues' enduring vitality, just as is the continuing presence of the "chitlin circuit," that venue of clubs and theaters, relatively unknown to white followers, that continues to book stars like Bobby Bland, Little Milton, Bobby Rush, Denise LaSalle, and other artists. These professional entertainers play to large, enthusiastic black audiences, audiences whose very existence undercuts the common notion that whites are now the blues' only audience.

No less active are the blues clubs of cities like Chicago, East St. Louis (Tubby's Red Room), Memphis (Green's), St. Louis (Spraggin's Hacienda Lounge) and Kansas City (H & M Bar-B-Q).

Chicago has retained its reputation as a major blues center not only by the continuing existence of its famous North Side clubs like Kingston Mines, Lilly's, B.L.U.E.S. and B.L.U.E.S. Etc, but because it stills supports West Side clubs like Rosa's and essentially community or neighborhood clubs like the Cuddle Inn, Brady's Blue Lounge, the Checkerboard, and Lee's Unleaded Blues. By now everyone has heard of Buddy Guy's Legends, located in the South Loop.

Chicago also does its part in keeping the blues alive by hosting one of the most famous blues festivals of them all, while San Francisco still produces the longest running one. Other significant festivals include the King Biscuit Blues Festival, the Sunflower River Blues Festival, and the Mississippi Delta Blues Festival, indeed, at last count, there were well over 200 blues festivals a year, including the exceptional European festivals like Blues Estafette that makes an effort to promote obscure blues players to appreciative non-American audiences.

But listing festivals is not the point. The point is that these festivals provide a continuing source of income to blues artists, while exposing the blues to larger and larger audiences. One segment of this new audience — a segment that merges with the performers themselves — is of special interest: black intellectuals.

We are not suggesting that black intellectual interest in the blues is, in itself, new, but that such an interest has grown considerably over the last decade. There are, for instance, blues performers like Chicago Beau (L. McGraw-Beauchamp), who has been carrying on a relatively unheralded campaign to expose black thought on the blues, and whose *Chicago Blues Annual* has been a high-spot of blues publishing. (*Magic Blues*, a blues magazine published in Chicago by Lois Ulrey, is, in spite of its irregular publication, another important black achievment in blues documentation.)

Documentation is a significant subject, since one complaint repeatedly leveled at leading magazines like *Living Blues* is their lack of black staff writers. It is worth noting, however, that black writing on the blues often receives little support. No one who has criticized *Living Blues*, for example, has mentioned that Chicago Beau's *Chicago Blues Annual* or *Magic Blues* was providing the specific perspective that *Living Blues* was criticized for lacking. *Living Blues'* own effort to publish columns by Willie Dixon and other blues artists has been ignored. It is my own hope that as more articulate blues singers continue to emerge — Corey Harris is a good example, and Sugar Blue is another — they will clamor for a written voice as well as a musical one.

Modern black writers, of course, have already approached the blues from various angles, beginning with LeRoi Jones'(Amiri Baraka) *Blues People* (1963) and continuing up through Julio Finn's *The Bluesman* (1986), Daphne Duvall Harrison's *Black Pearls* (1988) and Albert Murray's *The Blue Devils of Nada* (1996). One of the most interesting and inspiring stops along this path was Houston Baker's *Blues, Ideology and Afro-American Literature* (1984), wherein the blues was invoked as a matrix through which one could conceive the specificity of Afro-American literature.

But this status report on the blues is far from complete. As one would expect of a music so born of conflict that it would seem at once to be both oppositional and affirmative while exercising — at the same time — the most exquisite powers of negation, the answers to all our questions are themselves contradictory and conflicted. One reason for this is that through the blues of our times flow several streams, currents not always congenial to each other. The importance of these contradictory forces is considerable, however, and I have devoted an entirely new chapter to their analysis (see "Tough Times").

First, though, take a journey through this new edition of *Blues and the Poetic Spirit*. The bulk of the book has neither been revised nor updated, but I have made a few stylistic changes, added a few references, and moved several chapters; one has been removed entirely. The excised chapter dealt with a few select pieces of the blues literature of the time, and now it seems superficial, so vast has the blues literature become. I have provided this new introduction, and well as a new final chapter, "Tough Times." Both view recent currents in the blues from two different perspectives.

At the time this book was written — the early 1970s — I thought it was important to show how the blues represented an authentic American poetic voice, a voice that used the capacity for fantasy to kindle the spirit of revolt by placing the primacy of desire ahead of the claims of reality. As it did this, it gave us a graphic representation of desire's frustration and a stark and revealing look at humanity's lot amid the clamor of advanced industrial civilization. Further, through the progeny of the image, "the unconscious determinants of our life . . . rediscover their essential nature in the larger context of human emancipation." Can the blues still perform this function? Nothing could be more important at the present time.

Paul Garon
February, 1996

the blues as poetry

If a toad-frog had wings . . .
— Walter Beasley, *Toad Frog Blues*

> All that is worth existing is poetry,
> from the rich red lips of a passing girl to
> the love-song of a frog.
> — Nicolas Calas

THAT THE BLUES IS POETRY IS BEYOND DOUBT; THAT THERE ARE those who doubt this is beyond belief. But there *are* those who doubt this, and hopefully, by contributing to a definition of the essence of poetic activity and its ramifications, this book will render them, or at least their position, obsolete.

In *Blues Fell This Morning,* Paul Oliver wrote, "If it is true that the blues is to be heard and not written it is also equally true that the blues eminently deserves to be written about. Though it is fashionable at the moment to decry any suggestion that the blues has 'significance' under the curious pretext that such a suggestion destroys the spirit of the music, the fact remains that the blues *is* socially significant. Failure to appreciate what the blues is about, failure to comprehend the implications of its content, is failure to appreciate the blues as a whole."

Entirely agreeing with Oliver's statement, I would argue

1

further that as a creative activity operating on a most unusual level of mental functioning, the blues is also *psychologically* and *poetically* significant. This fact is indeed the inspiration for writing a psychopoetical investigation of the blues. It will be seen that because the blues draws on the same instinctual sources as other forms of human expression but persistently remains relatively unalienated from these sources, such an investigation carries with it the promise of leading to a greater understanding of the creative act itself.

Such a discussion, however, can never be far removed from the societal elements that permeate the psychological categories themselves. The blues is the musical and poetic expression of working-class black Americans, and as such it has served and continues to serve a specific function in a specific social context. It is true that in recent years its social context has greatly exceeded its original boundaries, so that the blues can be regarded today as a world-historical phenomenon, the influence of which — though already considerable — will doubtless increasingly make itself felt on the poetic sensibility of this entire epoch. As the poetic voice of a people distinctively victimized by the whole gamut of the repressive forces of bourgeois/ Christian civilization (economic exploitation, political disenfranchisement, racism, etc.), the blues long ago found itself in the service of human emancipation by virtue of the particular manner in which it deals with such repression. It is precisely through its unique approach — which is sufficient to distinguish the blues from nearly every other folk tradition — that the blues today strikes responsive chords in the four corners of the world.

There have been historical studies of the blues, biographies of several singers, and chronicles of the recording companies; there have been eulogies, obituaries, and discographies; and there have been several valuable sociological studies, most importantly the work of Paul Oliver, wherein the everyday life of black America is linked to the content of the blues lyrics. Yet aside from a few superficial hints in Charles Keil's analysis of the role of the urban bluesman, *Urban Blues*, and the work of Harriet Ottenheimer, nothing has been written about the blues and *the mind,* the blues as *thought*. The several attempts that have been made to understand blues as "poetry" have failed utterly, mostly because of their totally indefensible premises.

It is thus entirely justifiable to present a fundamentally new perspective from which the blues can more fully be appreciated. I have tried to give emphasis to those aspects of the blues which I feel have until now been almost totally ignored. But while the framework of this book thus remains poetic and psychological throughout, I have not hesitated to reintroduce social and political concepts (class conflicts, for example) when I feel that such concepts were neglected in earlier studies, and especially when they throw light on the particular emphasis of the present work.

Giving proper emphasis to the psychological determinants of blues songs, and their poetic implications, is not meant, therefore, to minimize the dynamic interplay of specifically social factors. While this is not the place to discuss the substantive nature of these social factors in the blues, it must be stressed that socioeconomic determinants, which have been pointed out by other authors, lose none of their validity by our unveiling of psychic factors as well. To suggest, for example, that the travel blues draw heavily on psychosexual forces for their formation does not reduce the importance of the socioeconomic position of the blacks, especially in the South, and the contribution made by this situation to the formation of a particular body of song.

In attempting to clarify the role of certain tendencies and themes that have been overlooked in previous studies, it is difficult, of course, to avoid the accusation of overemphasis. Trying to illuminate the thread of poetry and revolt that runs through the blues, I may be accused of ignoring factors which other critics sometimes find more assimilative than rebellious. The alleged assimilative tendencies in the blues have been discussed at length by other writers, even to the point of nausea: indeed, the presumption that the blues is primarily assimilative rather than

3

rebellious or revolutionary underlies nearly every previous critical study. But here it must be said that even the best of the earlier studies, judged from the methodological standpoint, reveal certain deficiencies. Oblivious to the laws of dialectics that alone can unveil the latent content of the process of social development in all its isolated contradictory manifestations; oblivious also to the dialectics of conscious and unconscious life as elaborated by Freud and his co-workers, which remains to this day the most validated and serviceable model of the mental processes; and oblivious, finally, to the principle of poetic analogy that permits us to venture confidently from the known to the unknown, the authors of earlier studies inevitably succumb, to a greater or lesser degree, to a sterile schematism or, at best, to a merely *descriptive* mode of apprehension which settles for an array of facts rather than seeking out the underlying meaning and movement. One would think, from the works of even the best of the blues critics, that such figures as Hegel, Fourier, Marx, Lautréamont, Blood, Freud, Róheim, Breton, Teige and Péret had never existed — and this is to name only a few of those who have, in the last century and a half, contributed most to the elucidation of the role of the subjective factor in history and of the complexities of intersubjectivity in social development. There is consequently a "one-dimensionality" in the existing studies, an effort to restrict the blues to more or less positivist and in any case hopelessly simplistic frames of reference.

Quite simply, there is much to be said about the blues that has not been said. Developing new insights as well as tying up loose ends and patching up holes can easily lead to either a disjointed mass of facts, interpretations and speculations, or, if one chooses to scrutinize the elaborations of other writers, a huge redundant volume, out of which could be mined, by the diligent reader, a few new ideas. I have chosen to risk the former rather than the latter, with the hope that both the reader's familiarity with the blues and blues studies and my occasional recapitulation of earlier viewpoints will mitigate the troublesomeness of the tangled mass.

Although the following investigation is in large part psychological in its focus, by no means do I pretend to elucidate clinically the "psychology" of the blues singer or the "psychology" of the black American. Nor do I propose to clarify every psychological contribution to a specific theme, even if the theme is one to which I have devoted much attention. I have preferred to concentrate on themes and tendencies that I find intriguing, or on those which without receiving the attention they are given here would otherwise remain obscure. This, of course, is another reason why it would be erroneous to view this work as anything but a *contribution* to the understanding of the blues.

The second chapter of this book is devoted to a discussion of some of the mental mechanisms that relate to our enjoyment of the blues. While this chapter will no doubt seem less relevant to some than to others, it is really a necessary prerequisite to understanding the later discussions. In addition, certain psychoanalytic terms are used throughout this book. *Primary process* refers to the type of mental activity characteristic of the unconscious; *secondary process* refers to more "rational" mental functioning, i.e., those levels of functioning associated with consciousness, reasoning, and so on. Psychoanalytically, *repression* refers to that process whereby something (an idea, a memory, etc.) is rendered incapable of reaching consciousness. Politically, of course, *repression* refers to various forms of punitive domination and external restraint, many of which, when institutionalized (e.g., in the family), become almost indistinguishable from their psychological counterparts. These concepts will help us understand the blues.

It is fortunate that the blues has so far been spared the pretentious and pathetic analysis-cum-death-knell of the academics, but it would be folly to imagine that the blues will remain forever out of the academics' clutches. The barest beginnings of the academic intervention are already visible — as a concrete, full-blown reality, it is scarcely imaginable without a shudder. Thus, in spite of the enormity of the task, I still hope this book will help rescue the blues from the total incomprehension which I am sure awaits it in academic circles. The blues has need of "academic explications" only for those who are afraid or unable to meet it on its own ground and on its own terms. I have not hesitated to make use, here and there, of psychoanalytic, philosophical and poetic instruments of exploration; but their use has been precisely to shed light on obscure mechanisms rather than to blind and immobilize the reader, or to force the blues into some prefabricated mold. There is reason to insist that this book is above all an invitation to readers to examine, for themselves, the poetic evidence of the blues. That is why, in the following pages, I have preferred so frequently to let the blues singers speak for themselves. The purity and depth of their own testimony in the songs they have created more than justify the numerous direct quotations from blues songs throughout this book. In addition, hopefully the concept of poetry which, as an *activity of mind,* has been totally ignored by the same critics — so preoccupied have they been with outmoded theories of meter, rhyme, and the retrograde doltish snivelling of T. S. Eliot, Ezra Pound, and their ilk — hopefully everything having to do with poetry, in the most vital and active sense as the *revolt of the spirit,* will be clarified in the discussions that follow. Other dangers that threaten the blues, most specifically the danger of the white predator, are discussed at length elsewhere in this book.

In its social dimensions the blues has received a rather significant amount of attention; poetically, the blues has been subjected to the grossest mishandling imaginable; psychologically, the blues has been almost ignored. This present study draws on poetic as well as psychological perspectives, to gain insight into the nature of human creativity in repressive society. Yet the most specific perspective from which I will focus on the blues is the *surrealist* perspective — for it is surrealism that illuminates poetry today and restores to it its fundamental prerogatives; it is surrealism that confronts the whole dynamism of the creative process in a way that goes beyond psychoanalysis, beyond sociology, beyond all academic frames of reference, beyond all mysticism; and it is surrealism that sees a means to freedom and life which is truly *livable* in the fullest understanding of the poetic act.

The poetic act contains the necessities of revolutionary fervor which, for humanity, represent indispensable ingredients of the struggle for freedom. For the surrealists, this implies a dynamic fusion between the concept of revolt and the concept of poetry — for poetry is a revolt, the realization of which lies in the restructuring of human thought around the axis of desire, the refounding of analogical propensities, and the destruction of the ideological limitations normally placed on our use of language. Poetry, in the light of surrealism, also seeks to engage the imagination in a constant thrust toward other occluded aspects of reality, and through fantasy — that is, through the irritation of all latent faculties of thought — to awaken us to the immeasurable possibilities that lie before us, but which through the repressive structures of Western civilization are only dimly grasped or not grasped at all. Poetry, kindled by desire, is the light that can dispel the pallor of bourgeois civilization. It does this through its use of *images, convulsive* images, images of the fantastic and the marvelous, images of *desire*.

There is reason to question why the psychological and dynamically poetic nature of the blues is so little discussed. The answer, in part, is that the blues has only recently become sufficiently *popular* to attract attention from psychologists, professors of English, or other specialists in hindsight. Non-academics perhaps feel that psychological and poetic investigations are still the exclusive province of academia. The sadness of this state of affairs makes it no less true. Perhaps this is a good place to recall that the most revolutionary and far-reaching thinkers of the past century — let us cite only Marx, Freud and the surrealists — worked outside (and in opposition to) the cloistered milieu of the university. The surrealists, particularly, have consistently fought to destroy the web of mystification that obscures the processes of creativity and to demolish the conception that bourgeois ideology, with its infamous obsession with "talent," provides the only *criteria* for exploration. The task is difficult, but one must harbor only the most fervent distrust for those who feel it will not be accomplished. Regarding the blues, the surrealist movement has already made its position clear:

> Surrealism will demonstrate why the blues singers Robert Johnson and Peetie Wheatstraw are greater poets than T. S. Eliot or Robert Frost or Karl Shapiro or Allen Ginsberg. . . . (Rosemont, 1968).

This book is a contribution to that demonstration.

notes on the psychology of enjoyment

. . . and the blues'll make you happy, too.
— Joe Turner LP title

> For a man to be continually in
> pleasure, he must have the faculties of
> pleasure awake: to have a monotony
> of pleasure is still pleasant.
> — Benjamin Paul Blood

FROM THE OUTSET, WE MUST EMPHASIZE OUR IRRITATION AT the lack of understanding we have of the specific emotional meaning of music. No one has been able to explain why certain melodies are more appealing than others, why the blues actually sounds "blue," aside from obscure cultural connotations (or if, indeed, it does at all), why certain instruments appeal to some people and not to others. With only the most minor exceptions, these mysteries remain unsolved, but there are a number of closely related areas to which we will be immediately drawn.

It has often been pointed out that the blues distinguishes itself from numerous other song and folk song forms by its predilection for first-person presentation. The blues is indeed a self-centered music, highly personalized, wherein the effects of everyday life are recounted in terms of the singers' reactions. The unique personal level of this presentation, however, intensifies the appeal of the blues to its audience as a whole; far from weakening the bonds between the singer and his or her audience, the highly personalized nature of the blues seems only to strengthen them.

In the blues this particular sort of self-centered presentation is well known for its capacity to present us with the most *uncluttered* descriptions of human life. Yet in concentrating our attention on the nature of such descriptions, it becomes clear that one of the intrinsic qualities of the blues, especially the lyrics, and in a sense one that pervades all levels of interpretation, is that it remains close to its instinctual sources, relatively unalienated, and unashamedly primitive. Wrath will no doubt be engendered in some circles by the introduction of the last term, but the time has come for us to divorce the word *primitive* from the pejorative connotations imposed on it by puritans and bourgeois apologists and restore to it some measure of its original vitality and grandeur. Whenever self-styled "appreciators of great Art and Literature" nominate the genre that we know as blues for membership in their sepulchral register, we are treated to the most preposterous redefinings, the most ludicrous hedging, indeed, all the most crass bourgeois ideological manipulations, contrived for the purpose of avoiding a confrontation with the notion of the *primitive*.

As an example, we may cite Sidney Finkelstein's *Jazz: A People's Music* (1948). In his feeble attempt to defend jazz against the charge that it is a "primitive" music, Finkelstein first suggests that "the word 'primitive' itself, of course, is much misused as referring to tribal man. Tribal man was a very great creator," and so on. It is Finkelstein who finds the concept "primitive" opposed to the concept of creativity; too, it is only in Finkelstein, and those who share his rigid formulism, that the contradiction exists. Further, to counter the charge that jazz "springs directly from the subconscious" (certainly a rather vulgar charge and worthy of counterattack), Finkelstein can only meekly reply, "Jazz is a flow of emotion in music guided by the most conscious skill, taste, artistry, and intelligence." It remains to be seen whether by ignoring just *what* is being guided, we have exceedingly poor dialectics or are simply begging the question. In the case of Finkelstein, whose "radical" pretensions are reducible to populist platitudes, it is probably both. In any case, his approach exemplifies the nature of the limitations imposed on us by repressive class-structure terminology. No doubt the general charge that Finkelstein hoped to refute was the view that the American black was a "savage" and that his music was worthless. His refutation, however, unfortunately obscured the vitality, passion, and freedom implicit in the concept of *primitive*.

Needless to say, much of the charm, elegance, power, and appeal of the blues is inextricably associated with this concept, and this very association has evoked from critics not only scorn but ceaseless attempts to separate such vital and insistent creative activities from those forms of art to which the sheltered bourgeoisie is accustomed.

Relevant here are the psychoanalyst Heinz Kohut's comments on primitive rhythmic impulses in music (1957:391): "The weaker the aesthetic disguise of such rhythmic experiences, the less artistic becomes the music, as, for example, in some forms of jazz . . . one might also question the artistic value of Ravel's popular *Bolero*. . . ." Perhaps the key words here are "artistic" and "popular" (and the unspoken "sophisticated"). What is suggested as a psychoanalytic fact is really only the author's preference for maintaining the greatest possible distance between the concept of artistry and the concept of popularity, for, of course, the relationship between aesthetic disguise and artistic achievement is not nearly as direct or as simple as Kohut suggests.[1]

To fail to see the complexity of this issue is not only to fail to clarify the appeal of those creative activities that are genuinely "artistic" and popular, but is also to contribute to the tendency to reserve the word "art" only for those cultural achievements that are not popular. One might suggest that the proximity of blues to its instinctual sources makes it attractive to those people who have not become far removed from their own instincts; similarly, the revulsion for the blues felt by the more sophisticated "art lover" is explainable in terms of the aesthetic disguise needed by the latter. This description would doubtless please the complacent art lover, but let us rephrase it and suggest that the people who enjoy blues do so by virtue of the fact that they have not *lost touch* with their innermost needs and desires, whereas the art lovers who find blues repulsive do so because of repression. Further, it should be made clear that the desire for aesthetic disguise that reaches such a frenzied pitch in the art enthusiast, and that passes itself off as sophistication, is generally only a reflection of a specific and extreme form of alienation.

Given this, we can see that part of the attractiveness of the blues is that it is indeed a relatively unalienated form of expression. In a sense, "unalienated" becomes a synonym for "primitive," and this offers a key to the fundamental revaluation of the blues, and above all assists our grasp of the level of the mind on which the blues operates so distinctively.

The whole debate, of course, raged and subsided long ago over the vast range of productions rather flippantly subsumed under the rubric "primitive art." Former generations looked on these fetishes, masks, costumes, totem poles, spears, and drums, merely as ethnological curiosities, artifacts of interest only to specialists in "backward" cultures. Frequently they were regarded as ugly, crude, obscene, and childish. It was the Cubist painters — above all Picasso and Braque — who were the first in Western civilization to recognize the *imaginative power* of many of these works, though they focused primarily on the purely *formal* values of certain African sculptures. Only with surrealism did primitive art become a decisive influence, properly esteemed for its extraordinary magical and illuminating capacity, and its *subversion* of traditional European values. It is significant (though rarely remarked) that the very first exhibition at the Surrealist Gallery in Paris in 1925 featured the works of Man Ray surrounded by primitive carvings from Oceania. Today the battle over primitive art is over, resulting in a more or less complete vindication of the surrealist point of view. It is thus only appropriate that the surrealists should also be among the first to champion the singularly exalting imaginative qualities of another realm of primitivism — the blues.

Heinz Kohut (1957) provides us with a great service when he observes that words and their meaning are comparatively superficial and related to the secondary processes; tone, he continues, is a more primitive quality and more related to primary process activity. We are reminded once again that it is the tone of the blues, the way they are played and sung (rather than the words themselves) that establishes the songs' definitive credentials most clearly. Thus, a blues song can be distinguished from a non-blues by the way in which the almost indefinable *manner* of the performance relates to primary process functioning; the words become secondary elaboration. The well-known inability to be articulate in this matter, the constant resorting to vague criteria like "funky" and "soul," all suggest that we are still incapable of describing, in secondary process terms (words), the nature of our primary process response to the blues.

While it would be futile to suggest a single source from which the "blue" tones of the blues singer draw their almost indescribable attractiveness, we can speculate that at least some decisive contributions to the force of appeal in the blues can be found in the listener's infancy: perhaps the soothing voice of the parents, or more likely, the infant's own crying. The crying as symptomatic of a painful state produces pleasure in the listener insofar as it can be identified with "from afar" — thus the aesthetic disguise operates in such a way that painful emotions can be recalled and mastered when listening to the blues, the aesthetic illusion maintaining the distance necessary for mastery. As speculative as this may seem, the hypothesis is strengthened

13

when we recall that the word "cry" is one of the most common terms used to describe the manner in which the blues are sung.

Indeed, is it not our unconscious recollection of that period of our infancy, so aptly described by Ferenczi (1913a:225) as the "period of omnipotence by the help of magic gestures," when we had only to signal and our every need was granted — is it not that period that is revived in the demands of the woman about whom Johnny Shines sang?

> My baby gets unruly, thinks she can stop a train,
> Hold up her hand, stop the lightnin' and the rain.
> (*Black Panther* [unissued version])

There will be few contributions that we can make to clarify the nature of the specifically *musical* appeal of the blues — most of this study will concentrate on the lyrics. But before discussing the lyrics of the blues, and that quality of sadness and loneliness which seems so irrevocably bound to them, it should be pointed out that the lyrics themselves by no means deal exclusively with such a restricted scope of emotional categories. The blues are also often joyous, assertive, aggressive, proud, happy, and optimistic.

> I met a woman in West Texas, she had been left out there
>   all alone. (x2)
> I found her ( ) cattle crossing where I wasn't even known.

> She fell for me, a raggedy stranger, standing in the drizzling
>   rain. (x2)
> She said, "Daddy, I'll follow you, though I don't know your
>   name."

> We snuggled closely together, muddy water around our
>   feet. (x2)
> No place to call home, wet, hungry, and no place to eat.

She said, "I care for you daddy, but I love no man better
   than I do myself. (x2)
But I have a mind to care, a heart to love like anyone else."

The wolves howled till midnight, wild ox moaned till day. (x2)
The man in the moon looked down on us, but had nothing
   to say.
        (Alex Moore, *West Texas Woman*)

May bad luck overtake you, pile up on you in a heap. (x2)
Well, you are nothing but a crook, may around you, now
   you know, death may creep.
        (Peetie Wheatstraw, *False Hearted Woman*)

I feel like chopping (it), chips flying everywhere. (x2)
        (Charlie Patton, *Down The Dirt Road Blues*)

You'll never get away now, baby, and all my worries are
   gone. (x2)
You're gonna wake up one of these mornings, you'll be
   rolling in my arms.
        (Joe Turner, *Wee Baby Blues*)

I'm so tore up and bothered, I don't even trust myself.
        (Mercy Dee, *Call the Asylum*)

I wish I knew how much life was mine.
        (Lottie Beaman, *Red River Blues*)

I did more for you than you understand,
You can tell by the bullet holes, mama now, here in my hand.
        (Peetie Wheatstraw, *Ice and Snow Blues*)

Be so glad when my buddy's dead and gone. (x2)
Lord, my buddy got something, now lord, I like to own.
>   (Mississippi Bracey, *You Scolded Me And Drove Me
>   From Your Door*)

Now I received a letter, now, from a girlfriend of mine
    today. (x2)
She said now she could do much better, ooh well well, but
    I was always in her way.
>   (Peetie Wheatstraw, *Blues at My Door*)

All this is not to deny that there is a sadness in the blues, often in the lyrics themselves. But that we enjoy these songs seems to be taken for granted, and if one were to seek the nature of the psychic process whereby we enjoy listening to the blues, "identification" would be the most frequent answer, for we do identify with the singer of a song. Yet it's easier to understand how we gain pleasure by identifying with an artist who is singing of his or her happiness, for through identification, the singer's joy becomes ours. How is it that we gain definite pleasure by identifying with the singer's sadness? And do we gain this pleasure through identification, in its psychoanalytic sense, or through other mechanisms? A clarification of this problem is essential if we are to understand how and why we enjoy the blues.

A clinical definition of identification will help bring its function into focus. Abbreviating a definition of R. Schafer's (1968:155), we can say "through identification, the subject . . . represents as his own one or more . . . characteristics of the object . . ." Schafer feels that the highest level of identification is *generative empathy*, in which the subject "feels what the object feels; and yet, above all, out of self-interest as well as interest in the object, he maintains his individuality and perspective at the same time." As we are used to understanding identification (psychoanalytically) as a process that contributes to super-ego formation and the resolution of conflicts associated with certain states of infancy, it should be pointed out that the process can take place during other periods of life, at other levels, and may be based on the smallest characteristic(s) of an object.[2]

With a better understanding of identification, we need only expand our discussion of the aesthetic illusion in order to enhance our grasp of the "pleasure in the unpleasant," as another psychoanalyst, Ernst Kris (1952:45–46), has put it. Kris has done much to develop the theory of the aesthetic illusion, and his elaboration is worth summarizing here. The unpleasant in art is experienced as pleasurable because the aesthetic illusion acts as a protective device. To illustrate this, Kris offers a curious anecdote, "a reliable account which reached me during the Second World War. A captain of a marine detachment on one of the Pacific Islands heard from one of the outposts a dim noise of voices. Though the enemy was at safe distance, a gathering of several men required the captain's attention.

"He approached the spot and found one of his men with a radio set tuned in to an American short-wave station. . . . [The captain] found himself within a short time engrossed in the story: it dealt with outposts of marine detachments waiting on a Pacific Island for a Japanese attack. No clearer example of 'vicarious participation' is known to me. Safety in the aesthetic illusion protects from the danger in reality."

Kris further argues that the pleasure in the aesthetic illusion is a double one, in both discharge and control (mastery) of repressed material. Pleasure is gained in "freedom from guilt, since it is not our own fantasy. . . . The maintenance of the aesthetic illusion stimulates the rise of feelings which we might otherwise not permit ourselves, since they lead to our own personal conflicts. It allows in addition for intensities of reaction which, without this protection, many individuals are unwilling to admit to themselves. . . ." Related to this last remark is the less refined concept of catharsis, which also through identification and maintenance of the aesthetic illusion in the blues enables us to rid ourselves of our own tension and unhappiness. Of course, connected intimately with this is not only the pleasure in catharsis, but also the pleasure in discharge and mastery of the same repressed material. In the blues, then, through identification and with the protection of the aesthetic illusion, we are able to discharge and master our own painful emotions, emotions often associated with repressed material — and this process of discharge and mastery is pleasurable.

It should be emphasized, perhaps, that the particular pleasure afforded by the blues has nothing to do with the pitiful masochism exemplified, for example, by the theme of the crucifixion in the art of the Renaissance, or by the skulking morbidity characteristic of most "expressionism." The blues singer, like every true poet, acts out of legitimate pride and disdains the etiquette of humility. It is interesting, in this connection, to note how closely the blues singer conforms to Hegel's (1835:291–292) description of the "higher language" of tragedy:

> The hero is himself the spokesman, and the representation given [in this case in the songs] brings before the audience . . . *self-conscious* human beings, who know their own rights and purposes, the power and the will belonging to their specific nature, and who know how to state them. They are artists who do not express with unconscious naivete and naturalness the merely external aspect of what they begin and what they decide on, as in the case in the language accompanying ordinary action in actual life; they make the very inner being external, they prove the righteousness of their action, and the "pathos" controlling them is soberly asserted and definitely expressed in its universal individuality . . .

The blues, like other forms of creative activity, owes a large part of its appeal to the nature of repressed material, and part of what makes the blues appealing is the universal nature of the forbidden wishes it expresses. While these unconscious wishes are of a common and even universal nature, their preconscious, or secondary, elaboration may vary widely from individual to individual, as Jean Frois-Wittman (1927), a psychoanalyst sympathetic to surrealism, pointed out in his discussion of modern art. Thus it may not be incorrect to suggest that at least on one level, the meaning of the blues varies greatly from one segment of the audience to another — especially from white to black.

Notes

1 In this connection, the works of the psychoanalysts Winnicott (1971) and Fairbairn (1938) are illuminating; the latter suggests that anything made for fun is a work of art.

2 Recent psychoanalytic literature has devoted much attention to the various mechanisms or processes of internalization. Thus, according to W. Meissner (1972), the specific mechanism we encounter in our study of the blues might be projection (and introjection) rather than identification; for the less understood mechanisms Meissner suggests the term "identificatory processes." Certainly we are incapable here of resolving a metapsychological debate that remains unsettled among psychoanalytic ego psychologists themselves. By abbreviating Schafer's definition we draw close to the original (and vague) usage proposed earlier by Freud, and it is in this sense that we use the term *identification*.

whites versus blacks

I don't see why white folks don't have no
blues — they got all cash money and
brownskin women, too.
— T. C. Johnson, *J. C. Johnson's Blues*

Why are all blacklists white?
— Bob Kaufman

THERE HAS BEEN NO LACK OF OBSERVERS TO POINT OUT THAT
the blues is becoming diluted, yet often this term has been used
to denote what has simply been a process of development.
Thus, I would not suggest the term "dilution" as an accurate
description of the processes that affected the evolution of the
blues from its vintage Delta recording years in the late 1920s
(Charlie Patton, Tommy Johnson, etc.) to the emergence in
Chicago of Muddy Waters and Howlin' Wolf, *c.* 1950. The
blues has continued to evolve since 1950 as well, but the most
recent signs of alarm refer not simply to evolution, but to a
process which has no doubt effected the blues at every stage of
its development, but now seems to take on enormous influence
and proportions. "Dilution," then, becomes specifically relevant
to the influence of the white music tradition in its most recent
manifestations, and refers to the damage wrought by the white

performers as well as the white enthusiasts.

Those who feel that the influence of white music has been extensive but not damaging might point out that at least since 1910, black music has been played by hundreds of white imitators, from the "jazz age" through the swing era and into the present decade, without having effected monumental changes in the blues' enduring vitality. As there have been white imitators, there have also been black musicians who have offered material that could no longer be called strictly blues, in spite of their having derived from a blues tradition: John Hurt and Snooks Eaglin are two examples, regardless of their stylistic dissimilarities. Am I suggesting that each of these men in his own era (Hurt from the '20s through the '60s, Eaglin in the '50s and '60s) indicates a weakening or a dilution of the blues?

It would be stretching the point to suggest that the *existence* of the songster (as we might loosely label Hurt and Eaglin) threatened the future of the blues artist. For one thing, it may be that a number of the blues musicians who were active before the blues as we know it evolved were originally "songsters," becoming "blues singers" only later. Some critics feel that in daily life, outside the recording studio, those artists whom we know as "blues" singers from their recordings may have relied on material more befitting the songster. This suggestion is countered somewhat by David Evans (1971), who in his study of bluesman Tommy Johnson says, "In addition to blues, Johnson had a large repertoire of non-blues or blues-like lyric songs and many dance tunes. The latter were played mainly for whites since Negroes danced to blues." The non-blues material in a bluesman's repertoire hints at his associations with whites, i.e., his white influences. Of course, a moment's thought reveals that the distinction to be made between a blues singer and a songster is quite a complex and dynamic one, with most artists representing a composite of characteristics that increases the complexity of the issue. Still, distinctions can be made. Anyone familiar with the work of Mance Lipscomb, John Hurt, Snooks Eaglin or

Leadbelly would understand that in spite of the varying levels of mastery of the blues, as a distinct form, displayed by these artists, they are more songsters than bluesmen. In the same fashion, in spite of the propensity of certain blues singers to include "popular" material in their repertoires, some artists are more clearly bluesmen than songsters: Kokomo Arnold, Peetie Wheatstraw, and Leroy Carr are excellent examples.

Yet it is my feeling that while the blues singer and the songster coexisted for many years, and in some instances the two functions may have been handled by a single artist, the songster at least signalled the beginning of an assimilative process that would eventually have more dire effects on the blues singers' future. No doubt the blues has always undergone a more or less continuous commercialization since its very inception, but my hypothesis suggests a quantitative phenomenon which has begun to display qualitative effects in the last decade. The blues singer is more and more becoming the songster. For specific reasons, perhaps no different from those that were operative forty or fifty years ago, the process has undergone a certain magnification which compels our attention. The songster is the effect, not the cause.

While others have made roughly this same observation, often with a keen sense of the contributing factors, there have been some whose insight is quite accidental, a result of poor exposure more than clear comprehension. Thus, several years ago, blues fans and journalists from Europe visiting Chicago declared that "the blues are dead in Chicago" before even visiting any of Chicago's blues clubs on the South and West Side or Maxwell Street. Poor Hound Dog Taylor! Poor Carey Bell! Poor J. B. Hutto! Poor Eddie Taylor! With fewer and fewer black musicians relying on blues-singing to make their living, one would hope that those who are still doing so would at least be recognized.

But why are fewer and fewer blues singers around? Why does there come a time when it is difficult to discern a Junior Wells

John Littlejohn *(right),* **one of the great blues artists; he's shown here, with Eddie Shaw, at Big Duke's Blue Flame Lounge on West Madison Street in Chicago.**

or /a Buddy Guy performance from a James Brown performance? And why does a really first-rate bluesman like Howlin' Wolf find himself represented on an album called "Message to the Young," an album which in every respect is garbage? Why, indeed?

The ultimate answers to these questions are to be found, of course, in the all-pervasive encroachments of the vast modern industrial reorganization developed during and after World War II. Black workers are no longer in any sense a "peripheral" subcategory of the American working class. Their crucial position in heavy industry today, as well as in the so-called service industries (the post office, municipal transport) gives them a revolutionary potential far exceeding that of any sector of the workforce in U.S. history. The large-scale black insurrections that convulsed the United States a few years ago, in Watts, Philadelphia, Chicago, Newark, Detroit and numerous other cities, convey an idea of the black population's changed mood as a result of its social transformation from a rural proletariat into a largely urbanized and industrial proletariat. These changes, like all rapid and sweeping social changes, have inevitably produced a great deal of disorientation and bewilderment, not only among the older people who attained maturity in far different conditions, but also among the youth. Observing their parents' bewilderment, and noting how so many older values seem no longer to apply, black youths often become unsure of their own roots, their own "identity," as it is said, and consequently their own real capacities. The recent fad, throughout U.S. black ghettoes, for Muslim paraphernalia and for African items generally, reflects the same disorientation and confusion that has sent hordes of white U.S. youths into retrograde and ridiculous fads such as communes, Maoism, macrobiotic diets, and crackpot psychotherapies. The "official" values, and the institutions upholding them, have collapsed; all those who no longer expect anything from the existing order have begun the arduous search for solutions outside the prevailing frameworks. The dialectics of the social process, of course, preclude any simple-minded formulism in this regard; sometimes an intrinsically worthless doctrine or trend can provide a point of departure for truly significant developments. Malcolm X, for example, began formulating his critique of the repressive structure of advanced industrial society as a member of the Black Muslims; even the commercial fetishization of African artifacts in one sector of the black intelligentsia focused attention on black civilizations and thus could be said to have contributed to a fundamental reassessment of the course of world history.[1]

What must be emphasized, however, is that this process has

left very little unchanged. The smallest details of everyday life —
dress, hair styles, argot — differ drastically from what they were
ten or twenty years ago. Not even the blues — or perhaps we
should say *especially* not the blues, which for decades has been
the most sensitive seismograph recording every tremor of the
black population — has been able to remain above the fray. The
blues singer — proud and arrogant, sure of himself or herself,
relatively immune to the more absurd bourgeois conventions, a
free agent, indifferent and even hostile to the Protestant ethic and
the repressive myths of "responsibility" — the blues singer no
longer holds the same position in black society as he or she
enjoyed in bygone years. Moreover, those blacks for whom the
postwar reorganization of industry has fostered the illusion of
"making it," of becoming "integrated" into the acquisitive "con-
spicuous consumption" society; those who constitute the
minuscule, pathetic but nonetheless voluble would-be "black
bourgeoisie" (and not a few of their dupes among the ranks of
black labor) are altogether ready to find the blues singer an
anachronism, an "embarrassing" relic of a heritage they would
prefer to deny. This small *ersatz* bourgeoisie — an insignificant
social force compared to the white bourgeoisie — nonetheless
wields an *ideological* influence in the ghetto entirely out of pro-
portion to its real strength or historical destiny. It is in immediate control of most of the black press, the black radio stations,
black advertising, many black studies programs at universities,
almost all the channels of "black culture" — I say *immediate* control because in truth this parasitical sector is merely carrying out
the orders of the Rockefellers and the Duponts. These black
bureaucrats pretend that the blues singers are archaic, obsoles-
cent, left behind, etc. But the blues singer appears lost at sea only
to those who mistakenly believe that they've set foot on dry
land. For ideologues of black capitalism the blues is above all a
blunt reminder that their pretensions are only pretensions and
that their days are numbered. The slick, dishonest maneuvering
of these hired lackeys contrasts sharply with the resonant candor

and simplicity of the blues. A rude awakening is in store for those who look down on the blues as "ancient history," those who, as Big Bill Broonzy said, "got the blues and don't know it."

Therefore the (hopefully temporary) isolation of the blues singer from the black community during the uninspiring heyday of Motown and "soul" in no way mitigates the revolutionary poetic character of the blues. I think it was Muddy Waters who said "the boogaloo ain't gonna make no history."

It is no less plain that the "soul" market, with its younger and more responsive audience, presents the young lower-class black musician with a temptation that is hard to resist. Some bluesmen, such as Otis Rush, have always considered soul and R&B hits as potential sources of repertoire without thereby totally sacrificing their role as bluesmen. Other blues singers are coming to rely more and more on R&B material; we must admit the possibility that many young black musicians begin as soul performers today when twenty years ago they might have become *blues* singers. The declining popularity of the blues is inseparable from the rise of the "soul" phenomenon; but the question remains, why has the blues declined in popularity in the black community?

The answer lies, as I have suggested, in the *contradictory* development of ghetto culture throughout the process of urbanization and industrialization. The black workers' assumption of a decisive strategic position at the point of industrial production is accompanied often by a contradictory accommodation, on the plane of everyday life — and under the tutelage of the "black bourgeoisie" — to essentially bourgeois values: one step forward, two steps back. The increasing alienation brought about by the urbanization process leads to the creation of a false "need" for a less forthright presentation (in terms of the aesthetic illusion) than the blues usually permits. The unhappy effort to adapt to what seems to be a more "civilized" (alienated) standard implies the rejection of one's own ("uncivilized") desires. The increasing alienation carries with it, rather explicitly, I think, an estrangement from the blues, for the blues is above all a vehicle of desire linked closely — indeed too closely for modern taste — to the unconscious.

By alienation I am implying not just a "distance" maintained by secondary elaboration and aesthetic disguise in art, but also certain affective states related to revulsion, and in turn to anxiety; that is, to an inability or an unwillingness to recognize one's own instinctual impulses. It is this feeling towards one's own basic desires that makes the blues, in its candor and simplicity, offensive to the prevailing moral code.

Aimé Césaire (1972) has pointed out that blacks have always been doubly alienated and proletarianized, first as workers, then as blacks, but the blues has always reflected the incomplete aspects — the "loopholes" — of this alienation *for the black worker.* A more complete and thorough alienation, including a rejection of the blues, has always typified the black "middle class." Even here, however, there are exceptional cases that reveal only a superficial rejection — beneath a superficial disgust we find traces of a more permanent affinity. This is not a question of course of innate disposition, but simply one of public attitude and display. As blues singer Koko Taylor said, (O'Neal) "So many people, if you meet 'em on the street, they'll say they don't like the blues. But if you follow 'em home, you see a whole stack of B.B. King LP's, and Howlin' Wolfs, and Muddys, the whole thing."

With the rise in popularity of soul music in the black community, and with the corresponding decline in popularity of the blues, there has been an enormous ascendence in the popularity of the blues among young whites. There is little doubt that what have attracted the whites are precisely those aspects for which the blues has been partially rejected in the black community; in fact, it can be considered a minor "cultural revolution" of our time that millions of white youths, and not only in English-speaking countries but in France, Germany, Sweden, the Soviet Union — not to mention the non-white youths of

Japan and elsewhere in Asia — declare themselves ardent enthusiasts of the blues. Yet, while the intentions of the white enthusiasts are good, their effect, in the U.S. at least, could be annihilating.

Signs of these ill effects began to appear following the 1960s boom in rediscovering 1920s country blues singers, when the blues singers began to get more offers for appearances at colleges and night clubs. As the (white) public demand for blues began to increase, so did the number of white imitators. Often blues-based rock bands are paid hundreds (if not thousands) of dollars more than black blues bands appearing at the same clubs or festivals.

There is nothing really new about this, of course. René Crevel (1932:79), in an early and passionate surrealist critique of contemporary ideology, focused on one aspect of this phenomenon when he wrote that "for whites, blacks are only means — occasions for diversion, like the slaves of rich Romans during the Late Empire." As examples of this exploitative "exoticism" Crevel cited the success, in Paris, of "orchestras from Harlem" and "all the tom-toms of the Colonial Exhibition." Moreover, the phenomenon did not go unnoticed by the blues singers themselves — many of whom, ever hopeful of increasing their popularity as well as their earnings, began to play music which they hoped would be more pleasing to their new white audience. Just as it was difficult for John Lomax in 1940 to convince Blind Willie McTell to play real blues (as well as some songs fitting Lomax's peculiar idea of "protest music") for him, a white man, rather than that particular segment of McTell's repertoire which was reserved for whites, it became increasingly difficult to convince blues singers of the '60s and '70s that their white audience actually wanted to hear the blues; at times, it is doubtful if such an audience *did* want to hear the blues. I have said that it is difficult to distinguish a James Brown performance from a Junior Wells or Buddy Guy performance at a blues festival such as Ann Arbor in 1970; but when Wells or Guy are back in

"For whites, blacks are only means — occasions for diversion" (René Crevel). Ms. Hope Hampton, employees of Associated National Pictures of Kentucky, and a Negro boy. Louisville, Kentucky, 1921.

Chicago, at a black club, the clowning diminishes, they play more actual blues material, and they refrain from playing short segments of songs as they did at Ann Arbor. Most of the clowning, pop material, and song snatches are reserved for whites only.

If a bluesman decides to ignore the demands of his white audience, he finds that his own integrity means little to the capitalist predilections of the recording company owners. Thus countless country and urban blues singers have been recorded recently with the most ludicrous and degrading accompaniments imaginable, all designed to increase the marketability of the LPs, by capturing larger segments of the rock-buying public.

It would be silly, of course, to assume that in a capitalist economy the value (in dollars) of the blues at the point of consumption would not affect its vitality at the point of production, even if a case could be made for a less reprehensible commodity approach to art.[2] The record company owners who would make such an anti-commodity case find themselves in a peculiar position, for it is often their task to manipulate their performers, in a quest for "authenticity," to such an extent that the performer's authenticity is in fact abandoned, and all that is retained is its appearance.

As an example, consider Big Bill Broonzy. With over two hundred records and countless performances as evidence, Broonzy remained an "authentic" bluesman until the day he died. The bulk of his recordings demonstrate that his most typical accompaniment consisted of his own guitar, often electrified, a piano and, after 1936, a trumpet or saxophone, drums, etc. This was the instrumentation that he used for several decades in Chicago and there is little doubt that the music he produced was authentic. Yet when he was rediscovered by whites in the late '40s and early '50s, when he was introduced on stage as "explowhand Big Bill Broonzy" after living in Chicago's black ghetto for twenty years, it was necessary for him to play an acoustic guitar, without accompaniment (as he had done on his first records in 1927) to re-establish his "authenticity."

In a milder and more subtle form, this same practice continues. A performer whose tastes and ideas establish his authenticity (as a "folk" performer) outside a particular critic's or record producer's conception of the blues often must sacrifice his real identity in order to produce an "authentic blues" album. Thus, when the excellent recordings made by Memphis Slim for Vee Jay in 1959 were released on LP *Memphis Slim at the Gate of Horn*, a *Down Beat* reviewer rated the performance as poor; clearly, in those days Chicago blues were not "in" — solo piano was more "ethnic" and the reviewer bemoaned the fact that Memphis Slim's piano playing was not given a more dominant role in the session.

Rather than pursue this particular question any further, I would only like to mention that the subject of "authenticity" is little discussed today; perhaps because the blues singers themselves never cared and the white enthusiasts have come full circle.

Before discussing the influence of blacks on whites, wherein much will be taken for granted and go unmentioned, there are a few more words that must be said regarding the influence of whites on blacks. As a point of departure, I would like to cite a number of references made by Charles Keil in *Urban Blues* (1966). Keil ardently defends certain current developments of black music, most specifically the "slickest" styles of blues; popularity seems to be the only measure of evaluation Keil is inclined to accept, although he harbors no fond feelings for the most popular tendencies of black music — Motown, etc. More justifiably, Keil criticizes the "psychoanalytic" studies of Kardiner and Ovesey (1962) and others for failing to generate a relevant interpretative schema in which to present their clinical findings, obtained from psychological studies of blacks. Keil's point is that those traits which the clinicians found "feminine" in the men (process rags, a certain gait, etc.) are actually quite masculine and are culturally determined. While this is true to the point of being trite, what is missing from both Keil's analysis as well as his opponents' is a psychoanalytic study not only of such culture traits, but of the entire culture in which they occur.

I think it is justifiable to point out that Keil's characteristic attitude of relativism contains certain dangers. "Listening to the 'big beat' radio stations," Keil says, "I find it increasingly difficult to separate white and Negro performers . . ." So do we all. Keil also quotes a blues fan (black) who feels that B.B. King has made the blues presentable — "no harps, moaning, or shit like that. These guys have brought the blues up to date — made it modern. None of that nasty gut-bucket stuff." Of course, "nasty" is the key word here, hinting at the offensiveness of the "real" blues. I am not suggesting that B.B. King, at the time of Keil's book, was anything but a first-rate bluesman. But what was implied by Keil's interviewee was a growing alienation that makes the real "nasty" blues unacceptable. Keil also suggests that if the "ancient" blues singers who perform at the festivals in Europe were to appear at the Regal or Apollo, they would be hooted off stage. No doubt Keil is correct in his citation of this

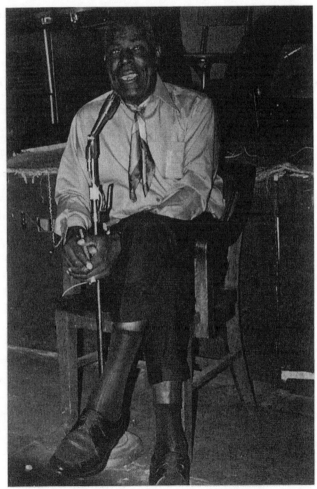

Howlin' Wolf: at his best, unbeatable.

imaginary incident as proof that the urban (modern) blues are what "the people" want; the old blues, the country blues, are unwanted and old fashioned. But Keil begs the question by not probing into the differences between the two styles — indeed, he seems to consider the question settled by the process of stylistic evolution and the demands of culture.

But the question is not settled, certainly not in terms of the poetic assault on consciousness. (My own personal feeling is that if James Brown has eclipsed Lightnin' Hopkins in popularity, so much the worse *poetically* for everyone.) Modern blues (which to Keil includes not only Howlin' Wolf, Muddy Waters and B.B. King, but also Bobby Bland and others) tends, in its most sophisticated performers, to leave behind the power of the image and the capacity of fantasy, and to concentrate, almost without even a glimmer of imagination, on more mundane activities. The subject matter of early blues was frequently mundane as well, but it was precisely the *imagistically inspired manner* in which such subjects were dealt with that singularly distinguished the blues from other forms.

Today the most modern blues are often lyrically indistinguishable from R&B and "soul" music in their increasing vapidity. Keil misses the point when he says, "A . . . factor here is historical respectability. A coarse lyric of thirty years ago has poetic qualities and historic interest; much the same kind of lyric today is considered frivolous and not worthy of scholarly attention." Keil is right for the wrong reasons. The truth is that it is very difficult to find the same kind of lyric today. The reason the lyric of today distinguishes itself from the lyric of earlier decades is that the lyric of earlier decades tended to be imaginative while the lyric of today tends to be vapid.

To avoid misunderstanding, let me clarify several points. By "the lyric of earlier decades" I refer mostly to country blues and not so much to the vaudevillian compositions of professional songwriters, which were, it is true, often performed by exceedingly fine blues artists, such as Bessie Smith and Ma Rainey. By "the lyric of today" I refer not to Howlin' Wolf, Muddy Waters, and B.B. King of the '50s and '60s, but to a larger extent to the music of *today,* the '70s, when the lyrics of even such stalwarts as Howlin' Wolf tend to be devoid of imagination, and when singers like Bobby Bland are considered by many to be the epitome of the low-down blues, in spite of their musical polish and lyrical sterility. B.B. King has, quite recently, begun to follow a similar pattern, using empty lyrics, a slick female chorus on his records, etc.

This trend has already been designated "dilution," by which I mean the increasing corruption by the whites of the black music world. It is easy to see that, except for a few performers, the blues will soon become merged with "soul" and R&B, and it

Muddy Waters, 1972.

will cease to exist as an autonomous current. That this may revitalize soul music is one thing — it remains to be seen. But it will be the death of the blues as we know it, and in a certain sense, the poetic assault on consciousness becomes neutralized.

While this seems to be the historical position of the blues lyric, the same cannot be said of black musical development as a whole. The diminution in importance of the lyric, and I'm assuming that its importance is directly related to its *power,* its poetry, has been accompanied by other developments on the non-verbal plane. The imagination has retained its rights in the field of jazz while it has lost them, at least lyrically, in the field of the blues. The experiments and advances of contemporary jazz musicians, especially those associated with movements such as the Association for the Advancement of Creative Musicians (AACM) in Chicago, indicate that the vitality of the imagination has not been forsaken. Yet the audience of ultra-modern jazz is infinitesimal compared to that of the blues of thirty and forty years ago, and this we must not only mourn but vigorously denounce as well. The effectiveness of white assimilation and amalgamation techniques has nearly destroyed one of the only mass-based poetic activities in the United States. As an activity of the mind, poetry lives on in jazz, but in different forms and in different ways, without the rich scope of the blues as *song.*

This is hardly the place to undertake a detailed discussion of the complex interrelationships between the blues and jazz. But it is certainly worth protesting here — or anywhere, for that matter, at any time — the current cretinizing notion that the blues is more "intimately" linked to rock 'n' roll (by way of the lamentable hybrid "blues-rock" and so-called "white blues") than to the most recent developments in jazz. The pretensions of the protagonists of "white blues" are assailed and, hopefully, successfully undermined elsewhere in these pages; let us here note only the insidious manner in which certain well-meaning critics and scholars, in this regard, play entirely into the hands of the most venal and reactionary scum. The fact that jazz mag-

azines, with *Down Beat* in the lead, have long tended to chronicle the trivial antics of rock 'n' roll, has certainly not helped
matters. But far worse is the tortuous argument of the French
critic André Hodeir, in his *Toward Jazz* (1962:62), that "the
spirit of the blues is not, *in the Husserlian sense of the term,* essential to jazz."

Hodeir is, of course, a "serious" critic; notwithstanding occasional lapses into hilarious pseudo-profundity, his writing often
stands in marked contrast to the frivolous, superficial, anecdotal
style prevalent among most U.S. and British critics. But the
remark just quoted is wrong, to say the least, and even danger-
ously wrong. Regardless of Hodeir's own intentions, his attitude
here, in its skeptical bad faith, reinforces the whole modern retrograde tendency to isolate jazz, to confine it to the rarefied
mists of a perfectly abstract "aesthetic" ivory tower. The much-
publicized "assimilation" of jazz into the machinery of bourgeois culture, which is supposed to have taken place in recent
years — proof of which, we are told, lies in the popularity of
such (white) musicians as Dave Brubeck and Gerry Mulligan, as
well as in the (posthumous) recuperation of Charlie Parker and
others — has been accompanied by vicious attempts to suppress
the younger and most revolutionary currents in jazz. It is no
accident that the young jazz revolutionaries have affirmed their
deep-rooted affinity for the blues. But it is also no accident that
contemporary ideology, as always in the service of repression,
maintains that the legitimate heir of the blues is to be found in
rock 'n' roll and "soul," and that the most recent jazz is the "inaccessible" exclusive domain of a small cenacle. The "inaccessible"
character of the jazz of Ornette Coleman and Pharaoh Sanders
— I cite these two because both began as bluesmen and have
remained imbued with the blues spirit in their most adventur-
ous explorations — demonstrates only the extent to which
bourgeois society has perfected its repressive techniques. As
Louis Aragon (1931:3) said, before his domestication, "Wild
beasts in a cage are wild beasts just the same."

"The vitality of the imagination has not been forsaken" by contemporary jazz musicians like Joseph Jarman.

Hound Dog Taylor at Florence's in Chicago.

As for Hodeir, his admiration for Stan Getz and, evidently, for Frank Sinatra, lets the cat out of the phenomenological bag: let us concede, readily, that the blues is *not* essential, in the Husserlian or any other sense, to the musical practice of these gentlemen. But then jazz, and especially the *essence* of jazz, has little to do with Getz — not to mention Sinatra.

On this matter Eric Hobsbawm ("Francis Newton") (1959:95) has said what has to be said:"The blues is not a style or phase of jazz, but a permanent substratum of all styles; not the whole of jazz, but its heart." More importantly, the jazz people themselves provide moving and incontrovertible testimony along the same

Luther Allison, another fine Chicago bluesman of today.

lines. A single example, of inestimable authority, will suffice
here: on the last day of his life Charlie Parker expressed his sorrow that "many of the young guys coming up didn't know or
had forgotten their foundation — the blues." And he added:
"That's the basis of jazz."

What I have been describing regarding the blues is a tendency and a transformation and not so much a static end-prod-
uct, devoid of any sense of movement or dynamism. Thus, it
would be silly to gather from my discussion that I'm unaware of
the existence of such fine bluesmen as Jimmy Dawkins, J. B.
Hutto, Luther Allison, Homesick James, Carey Bell, Hound Dog

Taylor, Freddie King, and countless others. It would be equally silly to assume that my analysis foretells the doom of these individuals. While the history of the blues is the history of the individuals who perform it, the danger lies in these performers becoming isolated from their richest tradition, and from the people as a whole, resulting in a total fragmentation of the blues.

This is the tendency of advanced industrial society, wherein any attempt at creative activity on a mass level is inevitably short-circuited and smashed. Thus, in a sense, the poetry of the blues meets the same fate that met most trends of American poetry in general, so many years ago.

* * *

We have now to consider the psychological relevance of the black man to the white man and what effect this has on the evolution of the blues. As a starting point, I would like to quote the psychoanalyst Richard Sterba (1947:416): "The male Negro as he appeared in dreams of white people . . . often had to be recognized as representative of the dreamer's father, particularly the father at night or in his nocturnal activities." Sterba also pointed out how blacks come to unconsciously represent siblings to the whites.

Dream symbols, of course, do not refer only to dream life, but are in fact one of the few indications we have of the nature of the unconscious activity that exists in us night *and* day. The dream is not the unconscious, but it gives us occasional glimpses of how our unconscious operates when we are awake as well as when we sleep. Individuals do not choose what a symbol represents to their unconscious, although they can in a sense choose (again not consciously) which symbol they may use. In spite of the multiplicity of symbols, those ideas which are symbolized are very few indeed: birth, death, the self, members of one's family, parts of the body, etc. Additionally, symbols have a universal meaning, not through "archetypal inheritance" as Jung would have it, but through individuals who create symbols for them-

41

selves out of their common experience. Thus, it is the common ontogenetic development of mankind (and not necessarily the phylogenetic development) that gives symbols their universal meaning.

Symbol interpretation, in spite of its being one of the few areas in which psychoanalysis can look to other fields (folklore, mythology, art, etc.) for confirmation, is considered by many to be the most far-fetched aspect of psychoanalysis. In analytic patients, symbol interpretation is usually met with total disbelief or disgust. Some critics feel that to interpret symbols is to rob life of its more varied meanings, for indeed what have we left if everything we relate to is only our fathers, mothers, sisters, brothers, birth or death? Perhaps no one has answered this objection better than the Hungarian psychoanalytic anthropologist Géza Róheim (1950:450): "I never think it necessary to emphasize the obvious. It is fairly obvious that a grown man is not quite the same as a five year old child, and that the President of the United States is not really the father of all the patients in whose dreams he might occur in that role. After Freud managed to dive to the bottom of the ocean, people now tell us that the ocean has a surface." And thus, simply, I am not suggesting that the black man is *only* father, or brother, to the white. Rather, it is an additional unconscious dimension of black/white relations, a dimension the analysis of which will, I hope, illuminate several trends that run through the "white blues" world.[3]

If it is true that the black man is unconsciously identified with the father by whites, we can expect the whites' attitudes towards the blacks to reflect this identification. It is my feeling that this unconscious identification contributes to certain tendencies in the "white blues" world, tendencies that place the highest premium on those aspects of the blues most divorced from creativity. I feel, also, that this unconscious identification with the father (or brother) manifests itself in relation to the ideas of success, competition, and fear of success, all of which may operate unconsciously, but which nevertheless contribute in large measure to the peculiar position of the "white blues" performer.

To be more explicit, numerous whites who are devoted to playing country blues guitar consider it the highest mark of their achievement to be able to play a tune, note-for-note, exactly as it was played by the original recording artist. I would say that in America, this sort of performer completely dominates the higher echelons of the "white country blues" milieu. Creativity, imagination, and improvisation are ignored in pursuit of faultless imitation. In contrast, those "white blues" instrumentalists who are drawn to the more urban (electric) blues, almost invariably do something to identify themselves to the listener as white. The most favored mechanisms are having the entire band perform lead solos at the same time; playing much louder than any black blues band; trying to jam many more notes into every bar of every solo; or providing a harmonic background or melodic lead that is of such a nature as to label the performance distinctively as rock rather than blues. I once attended a Howlin' Wolf club date with the members of an extremely popular "white blues" band. When we left, one of the band members approached me and said rather boastingly, pointing back at Wolf, "Shit, man, we play twice as loud as that!"

When it is recalled that nearly all those *country* blues guitarists who are imitated so ardently are dead, and that the majority of the great *urban* blues guitar stylists are still alive, it becomes less hazardous to suggest that, indeed, these unconscious identifications with blacks play a large part in the life of the "white blues" musician, and that these identifications make themselves known by determining certain patterns relating to competition, success, and fear of competition and success.[4]

The purpose of these observations is not so much to expose certain tendencies that may operate in the unconscious of more than one "white blues" performer, but to try to clarify exactly why it is that "white blues" finds it so difficult to exceed the bounds of stupefying mediocrity. Indeed, it's either because the

"White blues" started early. "Blackface" Eddie Ross poses on the premises of L'Harmonie Compagnie, Louisville, Kentucky.

performer finds himself bound (unconsciously) to not create, to not imagine, but to only imitate, or because imitation itself become slightly hazardous, and originality therefore invariably carries the performer outside the framework that can easily be recognized as *blues,* that is, outside the framework of competitive success. In exceedingly few cases do we find fresh, inventive, creative, poetic, original work which could, without the most irresponsible generalizations, be still considered blues.

In short, then, unconscious determinants, whereby the black blues man comes to represent the father or brother of the white, contribute in a significant way to the wholesale inadequacy of "white blues." Other factors contribute to this, to be sure: there is no doubt, for example, that through the same process of identification (with the black man as father = superior strength), the "white bluesman" gains enormously in self-esteem, thus reaffirming his masculinity, and so on. Also, it would be only slightly unfair to leave out the more conscious, superficial determinants, all of which have their own unconscious connections. For example, whether the young white enthusiast will be attracted more to urban blues than to country blues depends partly on whether or not the music that provided the most pleasure before exposure to blues was jazz, rock 'n' roll, rhythm and blues, or acoustic guitar music like hillbilly or folk music, from the Carter Family to Pete Seeger to the Kingston Trio. Again, of course, one would like to know how these earlier tastes came into being. Financial considerations also prevail since it's far less expensive to buy a harmonica or an acoustic guitar than an electric guitar and amplifier.

Yet we are studying blues as a mental activity, and a few words must be said, again, regarding the various levels of mental functioning, our analysis of such levels, and the reactions that such an analysis is bound to engender.

While a multiplicity of factors is responsible for the appeal of blues to young whites, it can be predicted that the revelation of those factors which relate to unconscious determinants and which have been revealed by psychoanalysis will call forth the most ardent disbelief, revulsion, and rejection. Similarly, revealing those factors which seem more "sociological" will produce no emotional response whatsoever, but rather a smattering of quasi-academic approval, for such is the nature of the resistances to psychoanalysis and the current academic fondness for "observables." Regarding the popular tendency to reject certain findings of psychoanalysis while willingly confirming others, Freud (1918:53) said:

> If we look a little closer, to see which group of factors it is that has been given preference, we shall find that it is the one that contains material already known from other sources or what can be most easily related to that material. . . . What is left over, however, and rejected as false, is precisely what is new in psychoanalysis and peculiar to it. This is the easiest method of repelling the revolutionary and inconvenient advances of psychoanalysis.

Psychoanalysts have rarely investigated black music, but there have been several articles by analysts on jazz. In one of these articles Dr. Aaron Esman (1951:222) suggests that the anxiety created in the bourgeoisie by the very existence of jazz (and, of course, blues) is due to "a return of the repressed — a universal source of anxiety." He goes on to suggest how the bourgeoisie defends itself against jazz in much the same manner as the individual defends himself against anxiety; by "reinforced repressions and denial. Many intellectuals rationalized their defenses by regarding jazz as an 'inferior' form of music, a 'popular diversion,' unworthy of consideration by those whose interest lay in the realm of the fine arts." To Esman, jazz represents "the id drives that the super-ego of the bourgeois culture sought to repress," a formulation with which I am in complete agreement.

It should surprise no one, then, to find that young whites,

infuriated not only by their parents' alienation and bourgeois mentality but also by their attempts to inflict this predominant mode of mental servility on their children as well, would be attracted by jazz and blues. To the ideas proposed by Esman, Norman Margolis (1954) has added that adolescents are attracted to jazz partly because it functions as a protest group and it provides group solidarity; its improvisational nature, moreover, is attractive as a means of free expression.[5]

To the above roster of charms we must add a dimension which is often considered characteristic of the blues: its open treatment of sexuality. There is no doubt that sexuality operates as an attractive force in the blues, and while we will return to this subject many times, it is here that one must give in to the temptation to describe one of the more lamentable aspects of "white bluesdom."

The male chauvinism that is so manifest in the blues is not without an historical base that makes it more easily understandable. Yet the "white blues" world, while sharing this historical base to a certain extent, could, with its connections with the "counter-culture," be expected to be in touch with other currents as well, not the least of which would be the women's liberation movement. Still, this has not prevented the "white bluesmen" and rock singers, in a pathetic attempt to reinforce their own self-esteem and masculinity, from borrowing from their black "fathers" precisely those lyrics and songs containing the most derogatory estimations of women's potential. Removed from their historical base and their socio-economic setting, these songs as purveyed by white adolescents are offensive.

It is exactly those mechanisms of interracial sexual dynamics, (from the aesthetic disguise to the father identifications to the return of the repressed) that make the blues so appealing to whites that also operate to make "white blues," even at its worst, more appealing to some whites than black blues. And just as some whites have always been attracted to jazz primarily because it is, for the most part, a music of black men, so there are whites whose personal requirements for pleasure, in terms of the aesthetic illusion and alienation, prohibit their enjoyment of black music. For many, any sort of association with black people becomes associated with "the repressed" and thereby prevents their pleasure, and for these people black music must be served up by whites. These people also supply "white blues" with its *raison d'être*.

It is tempting to explain the relationship between the "white blues" musicians and their audience with the phrase "Let the dead bury their dead," but in view of the fact that "white blues" has a rather large following, and in defense of those black musicians who play and sing the blues, as well as those who understand that the blues realizes its essence only through its fullest participation in the milieu from which it came, it would be pertinent to discuss one more aspect of the "white blues" world.

The most baffling aspect of the entire phenomenon of "white blues" is the legitimacy and relevance with which its perpetuators would like to see it endowed. This single fact is evidence of the cretinously low level of mental activity which is forced upon us under the guise of the creative process in so-called youth culture today (perhaps it should be recalled here that the very concept "youth culture" is a protofascist mystification devised in pre-Hitlerian Germany), for in "white blues" creativity rarely makes an appearance. Removed from the unique historical configurations that produced the blues, that is, the socio-economic and cultural conditions through which blues came into being, the melodic similarities produced by the white imitators appear trivial and spineless. Their audience is won through the interplay of several factors, most of which I have alluded to above, but all of which are supported by a monumental dysfunction of the critical faculties. Thus, "art for art's sake" becomes "do your own thing" while both adages remain no more than the flimsiest excuses for the perpetuation of mediocrity and dullness. As Charles Radcliffe (1965:133) wrote in an early critique of the "white blues" phenomenon: "The British singers argue . . . that no music is sacrosanct, that if they wish to play what they like and publicly champion, that is their affair. So it is. It is also the critic's right to assess their music . . . in terms of the Negro tradition and find it wanting."

The question, then, is not "Can whites play (or sing) the blues?" but simply, "Why do they bother, and who cares?" Since the subject of this book is the blues, and not its pathology, and since we have only begun to explore what the blues is, it would be senseless to devote any more space to what is, after all, only a symptom.

Notes

[1] For an interesting presentation of this whole question see *The Groundings with My Brothers* by the Guyanese Walter Rodney (London: Bogle L'Ouverture Publications, 1970), especially the chapter "African History in the Service of Black Revolution."

[2] It was precisely this commodity approach that many record companies operated under in the 1950s, when they produced hundreds of magnificent blues records. They continue to operate under it now and produce huge piles of useless trash.

[3] A dream reported to me by a young white blues fan produced much embarrassment in the dreamer. While he was sleeping, someone put on a record by Howlin' Wolf. He immediately began to dream of a jungle with large apes swinging noisily through the trees. His embarrassment stemmed from his feeling that the dream revealed hidden prejudice, but it also seemed likely that the dream-work had made use of this tendency to allow one symbol for the father (Howlin' Wolf) to be replaced by another (the apes).

[4] I am not suggesting that all musicians of one sort are victims of a particular oedipal resolution while other sorts of musicians are victims of another — this might be true, but the evidence is lacking. Rather, it should be remembered that patterns of competition are established through the resolution of the oedipus complex as well as through one's early relations with one's siblings. Thus the ideas being dealt with are present in all of us, and it is the specific way of dealing with these ideas, defense mechanisms as well as character structure, that attracts our interest.

[5] It's interesting to ask why psychoanalysts have almost totally ignored jazz and blues; as we noticed earlier, Kohut took note of jazz only to disparage it. The analyses of Esman and Margolis, however, clearly establish the basis for this phenomenon of evasion by pointing to the irreducibly anti-bourgeois content of jazz and blues.

imagination, instincts & reality

I done seen better days, but I'm putting up
with these.
— Richard "Rabbit" Brown, *James Alley Blues*

> Never lose sight of the fact that all
> human felicity lies in man's imagination,
> and that he cannot think to attain it unless
> he heeds all his caprices. The most
> fortunate of persons is he who has the
> most means to satisfy his vagaries.
> — D.A.F. Sade

THE BLUES DEALS WITH THE ENTIRE SPECTRUM OF EMOTIONAL
life, and not just with those affects that characterize loneliness
and rejection — yet, in the last analysis, it is the *way* in which
its subject matter is treated that gives the blues its undeniable
essence, in every sense *poetic,* and therefore far removed from all
literary, moral and aesthetic preoccupations. This is not to suggest that I am indifferent to the *content* of the blues; on the contrary, most of the material that follows will deal specifically with
the content of lyrics.

First, however, let us briefly consider the controversy regarding the blues singers' use of their material. The most recent

breach of poetic insight comes from those who, firmly resolved to establish themselves as social scientists by virtue of what they consider to be their own objectivity (pessimism), have claimed that most often blues lyrics are trite, mundane, repetitious and imitative, only rarely showing a spark of creativity. What interests them is not whether blues lyrics are true or false, but simply that they are dull and uninspired. In actuality, it is only the dull and uninspired critics who maintain that blues lyrics are dull and uninspired. The blues can hold its own. But clearly a literary balance sheet of this kind is totally irrelevant. The value of poetry cannot be determined by computing the ratio of good poets to bad or by compiling cumbersome graphs of arbitrarily classified images.[1] So let us be concerned with poetic creation in the blues whenever it occurs.

We must treat the same way the debate regarding the "truth value" of blues lyrics. The singers themselves hold every possible position in this matter. Jack Dupree, who recorded a number of blues about heroin use, was amazed when after his performance people would approach him offering him drugs of various sorts. Roosevelt Sykes, who became famous for his superb rendition of *44 Blues,* reported that listeners often asked to see his .44. The listeners assumed that Dupree's and Sykes's songs were contemporarily autobiographical — the singers say they considered this absurd.

On the other hand, other singers insist that their songs are indeed strictly autobiographical and true to the last detail; a group of singers associated with the area around Brownsville, Tennessee (Sleepy John Estes, Yank Rachell, Son Bonds) pride themselves on the fact that their songs are not only "well-made" but highly personal, related intimately to actual events in the singers' lives.

Still other singers also maintain that their songs are autobiographical, but nonetheless use much material that is common and well-known, almost public domain. Prefacing a song with a comment like "Well, I made up this one back some years ago when my woman come home and said she was gonna pack up her trunk and go," they proceed to sing a lyric that was actually written and made popular by another singer, often of an earlier decade.

Years ago, a number of critics treated the blues as if it was pure journalism, full of verbatim biographies and testimonies of black "reporters." Few cling to this position today, which indeed cannot stand up to the evidence. The latest reactionary trend has been to treat blues as "pure art," removed from its historical base, but attached, almost by substitution, to a false concept of poetry that should have withered long ago. (See for example Gruver [1970] or Guralnick [1971].) The dynamic nature of identification and the whole singer-audience relationship give the lie to the "truth value" argument — for the truth lies within the entire spectrum of black experience, and it is here that we find the link most firmly welded between the blues and the poetic act, at the very heart of the entire constellation of human desire.[2] For it is poetry that seeks to illuminate and realize the desires of all men and women. To assert the primacy of passion, to place desire above necessity, to place love and hate beyond contradiction; these are elements of the *method* of poetry in its services to the cause of human freedom. Thus, to insist that the blues is *not* poetry (thus Guralnick)[3] is to confuse the true essence of poetry — revolt and desire — with the craft of literature. Similarly, to insist that it is a "vast misconception" to think of blues as "protest music" because, after all, "Most blues unfortunately don't even deal with the subject" (Guralnick again), is not only to ignore latent content and human desire, but to perpetuate the dangerous ideology that it is only through "realism" ("socialist" or otherwise) that human desires find their most exalted expression. Revolt runs a deeper and more powerful course — if it is not recognized as such, so much the worse for the critics.[4]

But so much the better for revolt, for it is through poetry that revolt most enticingly penetrates the barrier of the prevailing morality; it is along this same sinuous path that the blues has developed as one of America's most stirring manifestations of poetic thought. To stem the tide of this revolt, or to pretend it never existed, is to ignore the human capacity for fantasy, perhaps humanity's most revolutionary capacity. Fantasy alone enables us to envision the real possibilities of human existence, no longer tied securely to the historical effluvia passed off as everyday life; fantasy remains our most pre-emptive critical faculty, for it alone tells us what *can be*. Here lies the revolutionary nature of the blues: through its fidelity to fantasy and desire, the blues generates an irreducible and, so to speak, *habit-forming* demand for freedom and what Rimbaud called "true life."

This particular form of revolutionary poetic activity gains more relevance viewed in historical perspective. The black working-class blues singer rejects and even ridicules the repressive norms of the white bourgeoisie, negating bourgeois ideology by the mere act of non-acceptance. Although this form of rejection/negation does not necessarily comprise an effort to change society's structure, it was, historically, the principal vehicle of poetic revolt for blacks throughout roughly the first third of this century. Other forms of revolt, although existent, did not relate to the black working class on the same level that blues did. Thus the blues has had a significant function in relation to black revolutionary activity today, for the blues singers' revolt served to preserve the critical function of negation during that period by providing a sustained poetic attack on the superstructure of an exploitative society.

It is certainly worth asking why it was that no ostensibly revolutionary organizations in that period "adopted" the blues or jazz in any way, or even considered them sympathetically. From the outright anti-black-cultural chauvinism of the early (and later, for that matter) American Communist Party, to the contradictory "nationalism" of such all-black organizations as Marcus Garvey's United Negro Improvement Association or Cyril Briggs's African Blood Brotherhood, the blues and jazz were ignored if not actually condemned. Thus, as poets with spontaneous radical inclinations, the blues singers did not have the advantages of even the slightest fraternal climate in the avowedly "revolutionary" milieu: they were forced to "go it alone." The question to be considered is not the blues singer's isolation from the revolutionary movement, but the "revolutionary" movement's isolation from the blues singer.

If we realize that a basic prerequisite for revolutionary thought is the supersession of "reality" (alienated work, surplus repression), we can see how the blues, in an even larger sense, can, through its assertion of the primacy of desire in the face of reality, lay claim to being revolutionary. There is a redundancy here, of course, for that which is truly creative and poetic is, by our definition, necessarily revolutionary.

The critics do not always agree, however. In *Screening the Blues* (1968:258) Paul Oliver writes: "[The blues singer] threatens, he sings of his violent intentions, but he sings out the action. In the blues he states the hopelessness he feels, and often the assumed disinterest. His response to the situation is frequently apathetic."

This is insupportable. To make such a mundane evaluation regarding the distinction between poetic activity and other (physical?) activity (which Oliver calls "his response"), between creative activity and "practical action," is not only to paralyze dialectics but to ignore completely the tidal magnificence of the image, its progenitors, and its progeny. The image — "a match that one strikes on the unknown," in Saint-Pol-Roux's definition — forces upon us the multiplicity of focal points through which the unconscious determinants of our life not only manifest themselves, but, through the progeny of the image, rediscover their essential nature in the larger context of human emancipation. Poetic activity goes hand in hand with practical action and the two cannot be separated. While it is true that the vicissitudes of repression maintain an ideological barrier between the two sorts of activity, at no time does poetry find itself incapable of penetrating this barrier, at least to some extent. The progeny of the image will no doubt play a more forceful historical role in the transformation of repressive categories into the new contexts of liberation, but this in no way dulls the historical importance, as well as the historical necessity, of the image.

Further, Oliver's statement tends to obliterate the role of revolt and the function of fantasy and imagination, the progenitors of the image. Beyond the confines of the reality principle, men and women are helpless without their imaginative faculties — yet it is precisely beyond the reality principle that nonrepressive existence awaits its realization.

Blues singers continually refer to sexuality and aggression, implying an intimate connection between the singers and their subjects. It remains to be seen whether the blues singer "sings out" aggression or sexuality. It does not remain to be seen whether fantasy and the imagistic tracings of undetermined ardor flow from the same fountain that gushes blood in time of revolution and produces more endearing substances in times of passionate love. The quantity of energy held in check by repression speaks against the suggestion that one must hoard preciously the libido that is allotted, as if its use in one functional capacity precluded its use in another. Indeed, such preclusion does become all the more true, the more dominated we are by repression. Yet what is repressed, and that quantity of energy expended on repression, suggests that it is only in fantasy and the possibilities realized by the image that we can recognize even a glimpse of our potential, should that mysterious quantity of energy become available. Until that time, the various allotments of libido and the evaluations attached to them, at least in regard to poetic activity versus "practical action," are by their nature nonhistorical, nonfunctional, and worthless.

EROS

> There is no solution outside love.
> — André Breton

Unlike the laudable author of the irresistible *Mysteries of Udolpho,* (1923:94) Ann Radcliffe, who "took to eating the most indigestible foods in order to procure nightmares for insertion in her tales of horror," the blues singer need not rely in the least on artificial stimulation for the production of *erotic* tension. The erotic tendency of life is always clearly present, if not always recognized. To those who suggest that the blues singers are "preoccupied" with sexuality, let us point out that all *humanity* is preoccupied with sexuality, albeit most often in a repressive way; the blues singers, by establishing their art on a relatively nonrepressive level, strip the "civilized" disguise from humanity's preoccupation, thus allowing the content to stand as it really is: eroticism as the source of happiness.

Humanity's preoccupation with eroticism is related to complex and multi-determined processes, but there can be no denying that while the sense of urgency and intensity with which we treat sexual matters is related integrally to frustration and repression, a relatively nonrepressed state of erotic pleasure would be pursued with equal intensity but with an urgency of an entirely different function. The search for erotic love lies at the core of the blues — indeed, at the core of all authentic poetry — just as sexuality lies at the core of every individual.

In those moments of most intense passion, be they imaginary or actual, the obsessive nature of eroticism makes itself known. This particular obsession carries with it a promise of freedom that is undeniable: love destroys repression. Eroticism becomes a paradox; a nonlimiting obsession. The obsession of love tolerates no distractions outside itself, but within itself it encompasses every possibility of human achievement and dignity.

The blues, as it reflects human desire, projects the imaginative possibilities of true erotic existence. Hinted at are new realities of nonrepressive life, dimly grasped in our current state of alienation and repression, but nonetheless implicit in the character of sexuality as it is treated in the blues. Desire defeats the existing morality — poetry comes into being.

Yet the blues is not only a vehicle for imaginative truth; indeed, as we have said, it deals not only with sexuality but even more specifically with the frustration of sexuality. The dynamic interrelationship of projected gratification and actual frustration is the key to the essence of the blues. Simply, what is possessed is not wished for — what is not possessed is wished for. If we see in the blues the promise of sensuous human joy and sublime love, we also see the repressive circumstances through which the wishes and demands of the singers come into being. The focal point for the projection of erotic pleasure is the frustration of the same pleasure.

The most recurrent theme in the blues is the frustration of erotic desire. This frustration, inextricably bound up with the whole system of class society, is humanity's greatest obstacle to happiness. Yet the singular method by which the blues comes to grips with this frustration enables it to be simultaneously reflective and projective in a fashion which enhances its liberating potential.

The capacity for fantasy becomes the crucial function in the ability to finally overthrow reality and the displeasures that accompany it, to unleash desire in truly non-repressive situations of gratification and joy.

The desires of the blues singer are the desires of us all — those who find the blues vulgar or repulsive find that the same desire in themselves creates feelings of disgust and revulsion. Nicolas Calas' remark (1940:391) that "surrealism after all is shocking for the people who are shocked by dreams" is equally true of the blues. The blues singer, like the surrealist poet or painter, often with an incredible array of the most startling images, and with a candor that is often stunning, creates works concerned with the most basic human desires and deeds. Poetry is generally the result when bourgeois/Christian morality is defeated by desire.

> I got a new way of getting down,
>   make the springs tremble on
>   your bed.
>   (Blind Lemon Jefferson,
>   *Bed Spring Blues*)

> If you can dish it, I can take it,
> I got to have it morning, noon
>   and night.
>   (Lil Johnson, *If You Can
>   Dish It*)

> He's the kind of man that I want around,
> Handsome and tall and a teasing brown,
> He's got to wake me every morning 'bout half past three,
> Kick up my furnace and turn on my heat,
> Churn my milk, cream my wheat,
> Brown my biscuits, and chop my meat.
> He's long and tall, and that ain't all,
> He's got to be just like a cannonball.
> That's why I want him around
> 'Cause I'm the hottest gal in town.
>   (Lil Johnson, *Hottest Gal in Town*)

In description of sexual activity, the line that might separate the allusive from the explicit begins to dissolve:

> She's long and slim, she's made up round,
> She can look up long as I can look down,
> She's a trucking little baby.
>   (Blind Boy Fuller, *She's a Truckin' Little Baby*)

Bessie Smith's *Empty Bed Blues* was a best-selling record in its day, largely because of its overt sexual references:

> Bought me a coffee grinder, got the best one I could find. (x2)
> So he could grind my coffee, 'cause he had a brand new
> grind.
>
> He's a deep sea diver with a stroke that can't go wrong. (x2)
> He can touch the bottom, and his wind holds out so long.
>
> He boiled my first cabbage and he made it awful hot. (x2)
> Then he put in the bacon and overflowed the pot.

While most blues that deal with sex refer to intercourse, oral-genital activity is treated in the same open manner.

> Bring your yo-yo, wind the string around my tongue,
> Mama knows just how to make the yo-yo hum.
> Bring your yo-yo, daddy, and we will have lots of fun.
> (Hattie Hart & the Memphis Jug Band,
> *Memphis Yo-Yo Blues*)

And:

> Your face is all hid and your back's all bare,
> If you ain't doin' the bobo, what's your head doin' down
> there?
> (Speckled Red, *Dirty Dozens No. 2*)

Hip Shaking Strut by Georgia Tom and Jane Lucas contains this spoken interchange:

> JL: C'mon everybody, let's do the yap-yap-yado.
> GT: What's that? Something smells?
> JL: Naw, you eat that!

Even disturbances of sexual activity are not ignored, as evidenced by this Lil Johnson song:

My man thought he was raising sand,
I said, "Give it to me, baby, you don't understand.
Where'd you put that thing?
Where'd you put that thing?
Just press my button, give my bell a ring."

Come on, baby, let's have some fun,
Just put your hot dog in my bun,
And I'll have that thing,
That ting-a-ling.
Just press my button, give my bell a ring.

My man's out in the rain and cold,
He's got the right key but just can't find the hole.
He say, "Where's that thing?
That ting-a-ling.
I've been pressing your button, and your bell won't ring."

Now tell me, daddy, what it's all about,
Trying to fix your spark plug and it's all worn out.
I can't use that thing,
That ting-a-ling.
I've been pressing your button and your bell won't ring.

Here my baby's all out of breath,
Been working all night and ain't done nothing yet.
What's wrong with that thing?
That ting-a-ling.
I've been pressing your button and your bell won't ring.
        (Press My Button)

And:

> Ain't no more potatoes, frost done killed the vine. (x2)
> Ain't no more good times with that girl of mine.
> (King David's Jug Band, *Sweet Potato Blues*)

The objectionable sex partner is dismissed in graphic terms in the blues.

> You're too big to be cute, and I don't think you're clean. (x2)
> You're the darndest looking thing that I have ever seen.
>
> What you got in mind ain't gonna happen today. (x2)
> Get off my bed, how in the world did you get that way?
> (Mary Dixon, *You Can't Sleep In My Bed*)

Disloyalty, too, is depicted in much the same fashion:

> I've been rolling, I've been stumbling, I've been falling for
> the last past six long weeks. (x2)
> Some man's taken my woman, I can see where he dirtied
> my sheets.
> (Texas Alexander, *Rolling and Stumbling Blues*)

Inhibitions are made the subjects of similar songs:

> Well, the first woman I had, she made me get on my knees. (x2)
> And had the nerve to ask me, oooh, well, well, if I liked
> limburger cheese.
> (Peetie Wheatstraw, *The First Shall Be Last And
> The Last Shall be First*)

The odors associated with sexuality play a significant part in the singer's imagistic repertoire; thus, Peetie Wheatstraw again:

I want some seafood, mama, and I don't mean no (ton of
   bream? turnip greens?) (x2)
I want some fish, oooh, well, well, and you know just what
   I mean.

I want fish, fish, mama, I wants it all the time. (x2)
The peoples call it seafood, oooh, well, well, all up and
   down the line.

If you love your seafood, you is a good friend of mine. (x2)
If you don't love good fish, oooh, well, well, you better get
   on some kind of time.

I want some seafood, mama, because I'm a seafood man. (x2)
When I can't get my seafood, oooh, well, well, I goes to
   raising sand.

So bye bye, people, I hope this July will find you well (x2)
Because this seafood I'm talking about, oooh, well, well,
   now, I swear it's a burning hell.
            (Peetie Wheatstraw, *I Want Some Sea Food*)

In this same category are the numerous songs like *What's That I
Smell?*, *What's That Smells Like Fish?* and *What's That Tastes Like
Gravy?* We will devote a special section to symbolism and
imagery in the blues, but even without the use of elaborate
metaphors, the singer can arouse our imagination with sexual
allusions:

What she did to me, people, ain't never been done before. (x2)
But she really made me like it, oooh, well, well, and I want
   to do it some more.
            (Peetie Wheatstraw, *Block And Tackle*)

A number of blues refer to homosexuality, usually with reference to "sissy men"; perhaps the most straightforward is the
1930 recording of *Freakish Blues,* by George Hannah.

> She called me a freakish man, what more was there to do? (x2)
> Just 'cause she said I was strange that did not make it true.

> I sent her to the mill to have her coffee ground. (x2)
> 'Cause my wheel was broke and my grinder could not be
> found.

> You mix ink with water, bound to turn it black. (x2)
> You run around with funny people, you'll get a streak of it
> up your back.

> There was a time when I was alone, my freakish ways to
> treat. (x2)
> But they're so common now, you get one every day of the
> week.

> Had a strange feeling this morning, well, I've had it all day. (x2)
> I wake up one of these mornings, that feeling will be here
> to stay.

All of the blues that deal with love and sexuality, and we have
quoted only a few, reveal the dynamic necessity of the poetic
destruction of existing morality and, by implication, the social
system that upholds it. Again and again, we will see how the
blues singer confronts this issue.

Yet in this matter of confrontation, interior as well as exterior
reality must be dealt with. Within the unconscious we find the
magnet capable of fusing the two, but we can assume a dynamic
unity of exterior and instinctual forces that affect the singers. As
the singers confront sexuality, so they must confront aggression.

The role of aggression is significant, not only because of its insistence, but because it, too, meets with inhibitions from within and without. Again, it finds itself linked to sexuality.

AGGRESSION

> Wherever you find injustice, the proper
> form of politeness is attack.
> — T-Bone Slim

One of the most distressing aspects of what Freud called "civilized sexual morality" is the inhibitions that result from the tendency toward fusion and defusion taken by the sexual and aggressive impulses. A most common obstacle in the course of love is the inability to confront one's own aggression, as well as one's own sexuality. The contradiction between love and hate exists only in the conscious mind, however, and in the unconscious the two coexist side by side and simultaneously.

The status of the contradictory impulses in mental activity explains the shortcomings of the sociological interpretations to which blues have been so frequently subjected. To interpret the blues solely as a sociological statement on black life in America is to fail to account for the numerous contradictions in the blues, contradictions that are understandable only in terms of psychic activity. The most vital sense in which the blues singers act as "reporters" is the way they become reporters of the mental processes. *Not so much the social or economic conditions of black life in America, but the effects of these conditions on the mind are expressed in the blues.* Thus what the songs contain may be "reflections" of reality, but they might also contain images projected with the purpose of overcoming reality.[5]

Aggression, then, is treated as openly as sexuality, often simultaneously:

Good morning, Susie, I ought to cut your head. (x2)
But I believe instead, Susie, I think I'll beat your bread.

Good morning, Susie, where were you all night long? (x2)
Do you think you treating me right, now, baby, you think
    you're treating me wrong?

Good morning, Susie, you heard what I said. (x2)
Get your pan ready, sweet mama, I'm going to beat your
    bread.

Good morning, Susie, you got good cooking oil. (x2)
But when I think you stayed out all night long, my blood
    begins to boil.

I know you're tired and sleepy, Susie, and want to go to
    bed. (x2)
If you stay out all night long tonight, I'm going to cut your
    head.

    (Lee Green, *I'm Gonna Beat Your Bread*)

A classic blues couplet goes: "I love you, baby, ain't gonna tell
you no lie, but the day you quit me, that's the day you die." In
sociological interpretations of a decade ago, a line like this
would be quoted to suggest that the singer might be a murderer
— clearly, this is hardly the point. What the line reflects is the
singer's open statement of his or her *desire* to murder. Thus,
every singer who ever sang "I killed my man because he done
me wrong" was not necessarily a killer, but did find it necessary
to deal with murderous impulses, first as a child and then as an
adult, the same impulses being rekindled by abandonment, disloyalty, mistreatment, and so on. The songs imply that such
impulses are not dealt with solely by repression.

Popular songs and country and western songs persistently
reflect repression in this respect. André Breton once described
the popular song as "a nervy little beggar who speculates on the
most syrupy and unworthy traits of the human soul." Hillbilly
music, in spite of some similarities to blues, is dominated by guilt

and conventional Protestant morality, and it is only in a hillbilly song that such lyrics as these could be heard: "Tell Daddy his little girl is so ashamed, but mama, I won't be wearing a ring."

While the hillbilly singer above has placed herself firmly in the grip of the absurd contradictions that are clearly the essence of middle-class morality, the blues singer Merline Johnson describes a different life indeed:

> I'm wild and I'm reckless, can't even trust myself. (x2)
> 'Cause my baby has quit me and I don't want nobody else.
>
> I'm going to the road house, way out on the edge of town. (x2)
> Where the music is soft and mellow and the people really
>   break 'em down.
>
> I'll get a man out there to give me anything I need. (x2)
> I'm gonna get drunk and gamble, and do just as I please.
>
> I'm going to buy myself a pistol, and hang it on my side. (x2)
> I'm going to join the gangsters and live myself a reckless life.
>
> I'm going to lock my cabin and turn my lights down low. (x2)
> I've got these reckless life blues, and I really got to go.
>   (Merline Johnson, *Reckless Life Blues*)

Indeed, in the blues aggressive impulses are far from stifled:

> I been talking to you, man, and I ain't going to talk no
>   more. (x2)
> Well, some of these mornings, I'll cut your head with my
>   two-by-four.
>
> I don't want to hurt that man, just goin' to kill him dead. (x2)
> I'll knock him to his knees, go back to the man I once have
>   had.

When I leave home, your other woman is knocking on my
    door. (x2)
I'm going to stop so much talking and raise heck with my
    two-by-four.
        (Merline Johnson, *Two By Four Blues*)

In the following song by Alex Moore, the singer finds himself
deceived and threatened by the vicissitudes of aggression —
with her anger turned inward, he might expect to find that his
woman "had the blues": but turned outward?

    I thought my woman had the blues, she looked so worried
        and sick. (x2)
    Only to find out in her bosom, she's carrying an old ice pick.

    But she wasn't sick, I could see trouble in her eyes. (x2)
    She wanted to stick me with that ice pick, Lord, and I don't
        know why.

    Half a pint in one hand, cigarette between her lips. (x2)
    Trying to get that ice pick out with her fingertips.

    Why don't you go to bed, woman, and put that old ice pick
        down. (x2)
    From room to room squabbling, every night in your gown.
        (Alex Moore, *Ice Pick Blues*)

Needless to say, the blues also deals with "aggression turned
inwards."

    Now if I had my old pistol, tell you what I would do. (x2)
    You know, I would kill you woman, oooh, well, well, and
        then my poor self too.
        (Peanut the Kidnapper, *Suicide Blues*)

I feel just like I'm going crazy, baby, I think I'm going to
have to commit suicide. (x2)
Oooh, everytime I look at you, baby, something happens
deep down inside.

I been thinking 'bout using cyanide acid, baby, but I'm
afraid that might work too slow. (x2)
Yes, I guess I'm gonna have to use, use, use, baby, oooh, my,
my forty-, my forty-four.
(Little Oscar, *Suicide Blues*)

Yet the blues that deal with suicide are only a small part of those
that deal with aggression as a whole, more specifically its manifestations toward the outside world. Peetie Wheatstraw, the
Devil's Son-in-Law, the High Sheriff from Hell, sang these lines:

Bring my pistol, shotgun and some shells. (x2)
Well, well, now, I've been mistreated, baby, now, I'm gonna
raise some hell.
(Peetie Wheatstraw, *Ain't It a Pity and a Shame*)

And Yank Rachell assisted by Sonny Boy Williamson sang:

Now run and get my .38 pistol, my woman running around
in a V-8 Ford. (x2)
Well, that must have been my woman getting away a while
ago, I heard somebody, Lord, at my back door.

You know I had a little trouble way down there at Tom
Wilson's place. (x2)
[*spoken* (Sonny Boy Williamson)] You better not talk about
them peoples, Yank, they won't let you come back there
no more.
You know it was just on this side of Al Rawles, it was right
down below May's place.

That's the reason I take my .38
   pistol, that's the reason I carry
   it everyday.
[*spoken*] Oh, You must be going
out bear hunting or something.
That's the reason, etc.
[*spoken*] I'm glad I didn't meet
you when you had it.
So if I catch my baby below
Tom Wilson again, Lord,
somebody sure gonna fade away.
   (Yank Rachell, *38 Pistol Blues*)

Numerous aspects of the singers' aggression betray the socio-economic base of their frustration. Creative activity never occurs in a social vacuum, but it is only through an abandonment of all theories of "realism" that a true understanding of this process will ever be reached. The dynamic connections between social life and creative activity are enormously complex — the blues singer functions as a poet through his or her refusal to accept the degradation of daily life. The essence of the blues is not to be found in the daily life with which it deals, but in the way such life is critically focused on and imaginatively transformed.

St Louis is on a fire, Chicago's burning down.
   (Jack Kelly, *Believe I'll Go Back Home*)

When I get drunk, don't nobody want me around
Always trying to turn things upside down.
Because this world's a hard place to live before you go. . .
   (Georgia Pine Boy [Joe McCoy], *The World Is a
   Hard Place to Live In*)

To some, recognition of the revolutionary capacity of the blues came quite naturally. The lyric below was quoted as a veritable

manifesto, both in the English revolutionary journal *Heatwave*
and in the American anarchist journal *Resurgence,* in 1966.

Want to set this world on fire, that is my mad desire.
I'm the devil in disguise, got murder in my eyes.

Now if I could see blood running through the streets. (x2)
Could see everybody lying dead right at my feet.

Give me gunpowder, give me dynamite. (x2)
Yes, I'm gonna wreck this city, gonna blow it up tonight.
                    (Julia Moody, *Mad Mama's Blues*)

HUMOR

> Through the adoption of humor as a
> conscious attitude we can assert ourselves
> over the confines of environment, reality,
> and in effect topple the whole structure
> and reassemble it as we wish, thus
> revealing a glimpse of the pride which the
> Revolution will restore to man.
> — Penelope Rosemont

Sexuality and aggression are part of mankind's primal heritage, but a uniquely human aspect of instinctive life is the capacity for humor. Freud (1905) devoted an entire book to the study
of the mental economy of jokes, and in a later paper (1927a) he
dealt with humor in terms of his more recently elaborated struc-
tural theory. His suggestion, oft quoted, that "Humor is not
resigned; it is rebellious" (1927a:163) only underscores our firm
recognition of the importance of humor in the service of human
emancipation. To Freud, the grandeur of humor "clearly lies in
the triumph of narcissism, the victorious assertion of the ego's

invulnerability. The ego refuses to be distressed by the provocations of reality, to let itself be compelled to suffer. It insists that it cannot be affected by the traumas of the external world; it shows, in fact, that such traumas are no more than occasions for it to gain pleasure" (1927a:162). Humor arises from the maintenance of narcissism in the face of disaster, and this description aptly characterizes the most eloquent and powerful essence of the blues. The description also makes clear the connection between humor and despair, a connection evidenced in the blues by the phrase "laughing to keep from crying." Yet this peculiar quality of the blues serves only to clarify this connection, a connection present in all humor. In the blues we not only see the connection between humor and despair, but we find that the effect of the humor is not vitiated by this exposure.[6]

> If I ever get from around this harvest, I don't even want to
> see a rose bush grow.
> And if anybody asks me about the country, Lord have
> mercy on his soul.
>> (Mercy Dee, *Have You Ever Been Out in the Country*)

The following verses are from Peetie Wheatstraw's *No Count Woman*:

> You fell for me, baby, but you only fell on my hands. (x2)
> And as soon as you get tired of me, oooh, well, well, you
> will fall on some other man.

> When I picked you up, baby, you was beat just like a slave. (x2)
> You had one foot on a banana peeling, oooh, well, well, and
> the other foot in the grave.

Some of the humor in blues is folk humor and, like the last line above, which is still used in conversation today, is drawn from a common pool of traditional references. Indeed, the same can be said for numerous singers; the verses seem to lie in wait, to be seized on by any singer who finds that the context of a song requires them. Also, they are often used when a more relevant verse fails to materialize, or when fatigue or forgetfulness temporarily obscures the creative process.

But the best of the blues are not simply strings of these floating couplets — often there is a fully developed theme, which, in the more comical songs, serves to heighten the humorous effect.

> I got a little woman, she ain't nothing but skin and bones. (x2)
> But when I get my big money, oooh, well, well, right to
>   Hot Springs she goes.
>
> Down in Hot Springs she will get 200 baths a day. (x2)
> And when she come out, oooh, well, well, she won't be the
>   same skinny way.
>
> Hot Springs is a place where all skinny people should go. (x2)
> And when they come out, oooh, well, well, they won't be
>   skinny no more.
>
> Now take my advice and don't treat your woman wrong. (x2)
> Because the woman that I got, oooh, well, well, she ain't
>   nothing but skin and bones.
>
> Skin and bones, skin and bones, is your woman's fate. (x2)
> Well, now, you better take her to Hot Springs, oooh, well,
>   well, now, before it is too late.
>> (Peetie Wheatstraw, *Hot Springs Blues*
>> [*Skin and Bones*])

Often the humor is found in *double entendre,* as in the Memphis Jug Band's *Cave Man Blues:*

Mr. Cave Man, doggone your caving soul. (x2)
You better quit your bad habits, digging in every dark hole.

You cave so much 'til you can't keep it hid. (x2)
You gonna get in the wrong cave, like Floyd Collins did.

You won't go to the barber, you won't even shave. (x2)
You know a clean face man don't go in no cave.

I'm goin' in a cave at the sounding of the drum. (x2)
And I'll dig and dig, 'til my good gal comes.

Got them cave man blues.

Or in songs like Barbecue Bob's *Yo Yo Blues No. 2:*

Hey, Mr Conductor, let me ride your train. (x2)
I want to play yo-yo, play yo-yo, play yo-yo again.

You don't let me on, I'm gonna ride the blinds. (x2)
"You wants to yo-yo, Bob, but you know this train, you
   know this train ain't mine."

I know a man, his age about 54. (x2)
Aw, he didn't do nothing but play with his yo-, play with
   his yo-yo.

I like to yo-yo, yes, both night and day. (x2)
F'some folks its hard work, but for me it's same as, f'me it's
   same as play.

You may be blue and way down in the depths. (x2)
Go play yo-yo, a little yo-yo, a little yo-yo will help.

When you hear them yelling up and down the hall. (x2)

Don't get uneasy, they're playing yo-yo, playing yo-yo, that's all.

I got a gal, she sure is big and fat. (x2)
"Let's yo-yo, Bob, because it's tight, 'cause it's tight like that."

I'm just a traveler, I got to leave this ward. (x2)
F'you want to yo-yo, mama, call on Barbecue, call on Barbecue Bob.

"[Humor] signifies not only the triumph of the ego but also of the pleasure principle, which is able here to assert itself against the unkindness of the real circumstances" (Freud 1927a:163).

Peoples raving 'bout hard times, tell me what it's all about. (x2)
Hard times don't worry me, I was broke when they first started out.

Friends, it could be worser, you don't seem to understand. (x2)
Some is crying with a sack of gold under each arm and a loaf of bread in each hand.

Peoples raving 'bout hard times, I don't know why they should. (x2)
If some people was like me, they didn't have no money when times was good.
(Lonnie Johnson, *Hard Times Ain't Gone Nowhere*)

The surrealists have gone further than Freud in adumbrating the critical, poetic and revolutionary character of humor; Marko Ristic, for example, wrote an important essay on humor as an all-encompassing revolutionary "moral attitude" (1933). The surrealist conception of a *subversive* humor enhances our appreciation of many blues lyrics. For often the humor in the blues is lodged precisely within the context of the denial and rejection of bourgeois morality.

> Some people calls her rum-head, but I calls her plain Babee.
> (Jack Dupree, *Rum Cola Blues*)

Sometimes, however, it's only a relatively isolated image that draws a smile:

> When I leave these walls, I'll be runnin' dodgin' trees.
> You'll see the bottom [of] my feet so many times you'll
>   think I'm on my knees.
> (Cannon's Jug Stompers, *Prison Wall Blues*)

But the variety of humorous references in the blues is endless. The richness and diversity can only be hinted at by citing a few examples:

> I don't want a woman who wears a number nine,
> I wake up in the morning, I can't tell her shoes from mine.
> (Charlie Campbell, *Goin' Away Blues*)

> Tell me, baby, who was that here awhile ago. (x2)
> Yeah, when I come in, they run out that back door.

> So come here, mama, I'm gonna raise some hell.
> You been boobin' it and noobin' it, I can tell the way you
>   smell
> So tell me, baby, etc.

> Well, I had the windows pinned down, he couldn't get
>   through.
> So here's his hat and his underwear, too.
> So tell me, baby, etc.

He come by me running, smelling like a garbage can,
With one leg in his pants and his shoes in his hand.
       (Casey Bill Weldon, *Back Door Blues*)

Now the reason I ain't been getting no calls, people, I'm
    gonna tell you what it's all about. (x2)
They tell me the Western Union man been getting drunk,
    he been leaving my calls at somebody else's house.
       (Sonny Boy Williamson, *Western Union Man*)

This song by Sonny Boy Williamson No. 2 (Rice Miller) is a classic:

When I first heard about her, I didn't believe what they
    said. (x2)
But I found out for myself that she brought life back to the
    dead.

She walked in that morning,
The doctor said he was dead,
People started walking out, crying, shaking their heads,
Ummmm, that's what his mother said.
She stayed in there 24 long hours and brought life back to
    the dead.

The little girl ain't but 15 years old.
[*spoken*] How you know?
That's what her mother said. (x2)
I found out for myself that she brought life back to the
    dead.
       (*She Brought Life back to the Dead*)

Sales Tax by Bo Carter and Walter Vincson, the Mississippi
Sheiks, begins with a spoken introduction:

BC: Say, Walter, we needs some cigarettes; let's go in and get
   a pack.
WV: OK.
Storekeeper: Hello, boys. What can I do for you?
BC: I'll have a package of cigarettes.
SK: Alright, here you are — be three cents more, though.
BC and WV: [in unison]: What's that for?
SK: Sales tax — haven't you ever heard of sales tax?
BC: We sure haven't. What gonna happen next, man? You
   know, they got a law here they call sales tax.
WV: Sales tax? What is that for?
BC: That's three cents tax on everything that's sold — they
   say that's the government's rule.
WV: The government's rule? Well, there's lots of things sold
   that government (doesn't) know anything about.
BC: Well, I'll just sing ya' a little song about these sales tax.

Old Aunt Marthy lives behind the jail,
A sign on the wall saying "liquor for sale."
You know the sales tax is on it.
Aw, the sales tax is on it.
Oh, the sales tax is on it everywhere you go.

I never seen the like since I been born.
The woman got sales tax on the stuff at home.
Aw, the sales tax is on it, etc.

You usta could buy it for a dollar a round,
Now sales tax is on it all over town.
Aw, the sales tax is on it, etc.

"I'm as loving as a woman can be,
The stuff I got'll cost you a dollar and three."
Aw, the sales tax is on it, etc.

Peter Cleighton, who also sang as "Dr. Clayton," sang these verses in his *1941 Blues:*

War is raging in Europe on the
water, land, and in the air. (x2)
Wooo, if Uncle Sammy don't be
careful, we'll all soon be right
back over there.

The radios and newspapers, they
all force me to believe. (x2)
Yeah, Hitler and Mussolini, they
must have the snatching disease.

Ain't gon' be no peace in Europe till we cut off Hitler's
head. (x2)
Wooo, Mussolini have heart failure when he hears Stalin is
dead.

I hope Hitler catch consumption, I mean the galloping
kind. (x2)
And Stalin catch leprosy, Mussolini lose his mind.

This whole war would soon be over if Uncle Sam would
use my plan. (x2)
Wooo, let me sneak in Hitler's bedroom with my razor in
my hand.

The song with perhaps the most amusing title, *I Heard the Voice of a Porkchop* is really more a minstrel song than a blues, but related to it slightly is Alec Johnson's *Miss Meal Cramp Blues.* Even here, the minstrel connections are evident.

Lord, I'm broke and hungry, and my money's all gone. (x2)
With a empty stomach, I've got to travel on.

Peter Cleighton (Dr. Clayton).

If I see a porkchop, Lord, I believe I'd pass away. (x2)
I ain't had a square meal in many doggone day.

All my crops were failures, couldn't raise a doggone thing. (x2)
I'm just like a beggar, hear these mournful blues I sing.

I'm so broke and hungry, I could eat a kangaroo. (x2)
I feel just like stealing, there's nothing else to do.

Won't somebody help me with a little bite to eat? (x2)
Don't care what you give me, I'd eat even chicken feed.

My body feels so weary 'cause I've got the miss meal
    cramps. (x2)
Right now I could eat more than a whole car-load of tramps.

In addition to its more ordinary forms there is a form of humor
that is excessive and even cruel, relentless and uncompromising:
this was designated *black humor* by André Breton (1937), and
numerous examples (by Swift, Sade, De Quincey, Petrus Borel,
Poe, Lewis Carroll, Lautréamont, John Millington Synge, O.
Henry, Jacques Vaché, Leonora Carrington and others) may be
found in Breton's *Anthology of Black Humor* (1940). Black humor
was defined by the English surrealist Conroy Maddox (1946:19)
as "a virulent satire and disquieting humor which as a deliberate critical attitude in surrealism challenges all forms of accepted
belief." More than a few illustrations of this "deliberate critical
attitude," which begins by ruthlessly obliterating the moral and
aesthetic boundaries of "common sense," may be found in the
blues. The following line is from Furry Lewis' *Creeper Blues:*

Mama, get your hatchet, kill the fly on your baby's head.

This is from Elmore James's *1839 Blues,* recorded in the mid-
1950s:

[*spoken*] Hey Joe, you know I'm a young man this time. You
    know I ain't seen my baby since 1839. I gotta find her.
    (What you say?) Hmm, unn.

Well, I ain't seen my baby since 1839. (x2)
Well, if I don't find my baby, I'm gonna lose my mind.

And this is from Mercy Dee's *Lady Luck:*

Lady Luck has never smiled down on me, I've never saw
    her wonderful face. (x2)

If it was raining soup, I'd be caught with a fork, people,
   ('Cause I?) live in this mad, mad Atomic Age.

I got drunk to forget my troubles, so (lushed?) the street
   cars looked like toys. (x2)
I flagged down the heat, and they throwed me in the tomb;
   folks, I thought they was messenger boys.

Well, they tell me not to be impatient, they say every dog
   has his day. (x2)
But I don't belong to the canine family, yet I'm beginning
   to live and look like one every day.

Or, as in this line by Jack Dupree, understatement offers a per-
verse emphasis; the horror of life in Southern prisons is simply
stated:

Angola is a place where you ought not want to go.
      (Angola Blues)

This black humor flourishes in the sub-category of the blues
known as the "dirty dozens" and its offshoots, characterized by
exaggerated insults and frequently sadistic sexual allusions. Some
of the most startling images in the blues are to be found in the
"dozens." For example:

Now funniest thing I ever seen,
Tom-cat jumpin' on a sewin' machine
      (Memphis Minnie, *New Dirty Dozens*)

or Louise Bogan's masterpiece of splendid outrage titled *Shave
'em Dry* which, in the following verse, combines religious and
sexual imagery in a manner reminiscent of the works of Sade:

Now your nuts hang down like a damn bell-clapper,
And your dick stands up like a steeple,
Your goddamn asshole stands open like a church door,
And the crabs walks in like people.
(unissued)

Further discussion of the "dozens" is made unnecessary here, however, by Paul Oliver's extensive treatment of the subject in his *Screening the Blues* and this author's "The Dirty Dozens."[7]

The humor in blues does not always reside entirely in the lyrics, however. Just as it is the way in which a song is sung that determines whether or not it is a blues, it is also the way certain lyrics are delivered that provides the humor with a means to its most subtle realizations. As in nearly every facet of the blues, it must be heard to be appreciated.

* * *

Yet, as we have seen, there has been much confusion regarding exactly what is heard in the blues. Some say the blues offers a realistic picture of black life in America; others suggest that the blues are poetic in the sense of meeting traditionally established academic standards. It has even been suggested, believe it or not, that the blues are a form of *religious* poetry, that is, "secular religion" (Gruver). There are also those who, threatened by the notion of an unrepressed Eros, would have us believe that we are hearing only undisguised "savage cries," and certainly not "art." We say that affixed securely as it is to the cause of human emancipation, the blues as a truly creative and poetic activity needs no further defense. It suffices to set forth examples, by way of illustration, of its vast scope and magnificent depth. Our elucidation of the blues as "primitive" is neither gratuitous nor demeaning; for we see in the blues a suggestion of humanity's original vitality and pride. Our conception of primitive merges with our conception of non-alienation. What we seek in the blues is a glimmer of freedom; and it is there, in every song.

This freedom must be viewed dialectically, however. While it is indeed the freedom implicit in the creative process, and as such, a potentially common property, and while one of the blues' most intriguing facets is its closeness to its instinctual sources, as well as its own particular form of secondary elaboration, the blues singers are also victims of all the repressive conditions that contribute to the degradations of everyday life. In their songs, then, we see not only an especially eloquent demand for freedom, but, once again owing to the level on which the blues operates, a particularly vivid depiction of humanity's repressed state. There is misery in the blues, but in spite of (or because of) its specific framework in black America, the misery is also our own. Part of the unique attractiveness of the blues is that it is through the blues singer that we are not only able to face our own despair, but can also demand an end to repression and insist on the erotization of everyday life.

That the blues singers present us with a vision not only of our unhappiness but of its conquest as well is a most crucial aspect of the poetic activity elaborated in the blues.

TRAVEL

> My sign-post fingers pearly with pleasure
> Will guide your eyelashes toward my ears my shoulder-blades
> Toward the open country of my flesh.
> —Joyce Mansour

We can expect to encounter both of these trends in any of the diverse subjects to which the blues singers are drawn, not the least of which is that broad body of topics which can be subsumed under the general heading "travel blues." As early as 1926, Odum and Johnson noted that . . . . the song of the "po' boy long ways from home" who wanders "down that lonesome road" is rich in pathos and plaintiveness." They devoted a chapter, not devoid of psychological insight, to "Songs of the

Lonesome Road," while Oliver (1960) dealt at length with the same material. Oliver's discussion was meant only to explore the relationship between the lives of the singers and the words of the songs; the lyrics were usually taken by him at face value, and as a study of the blues as a sociologically reflective device, his work is unequalled. Yet the blues also reflects a *state of mind,* and it is precisely this mental activity that gives the travel blues their great significance and appeal.

It is simplistic and naive to assume that the underlying motivation of the travel blues is *only* the singer's desire to go North and escape the horror of discrimination in the South. The contribution of segregation to migration as a theme in such songs should not be minimized, but neither should it be allowed to obscure other relevant material. The desire to travel is found in us all, for we are all victimized by the same repressive society, and it would seem that the harsh prejudicial system of the South operated specifically to intensify and revivify a desire which, under present conditions, is inevitable.

The most superficial psychological analysis of the lyrics cannot help but reveal that in addition to the colossal atrocities commonly perpetuated by racists, the blues singer also falls victim to the common ills of repressive civilization: aggression and ambivalence as well as the pall of white Southern bigotry drive the blues singer to flight. Still, we should not be surprised to see that here, too, mechanisms other than repression are operative, and thus through the blues songs we are permitted some insights into the entire phenomenon of traveling.

There is an undeniable sexual contribution to the pleasure in traveling, and this appears in the blues in several forms, not the least of which is the use of cars and car parts as sexual references. Trains, too, are seized upon for their sexual significance, as in this humorous couplet of Blind Boy Fuller's:

Well, the time I need you, mama, that's the time you're
  gone. (x2)
I believe you got ways like a passenger train, when one's
  getting off, the other one's getting on.
  (Passenger Train Woman)

Often the power of the train symbolizes the superior power of
the father, and it's the "mean ol' train" or the "cruel engineer" that
takes the bluesman's woman from him. This is not to deny that
many women must have left their men by boarding trains for
new towns, but unconscious oedipal and pre-oedipal conflicts
may be revived and the unconscious associations contribute to
the singer's choice of symbols.

It ain't no telling what that train won't do,
It'll take your baby and run right over you.
Now that engineerman ought to be 'shamed of hisself.
Take women from their husbands, babies from their
  mother's breast.
  (Charlie McCoy, *That Lonesome Train Took My
  Baby Away*)

While the flight North has been dwelt upon by Oliver and others, attention should be drawn to the fact that it is primarily a
leaving home; and for each song dealing with "leaving home"
there is another: "I'll be home some day." For what is left behind
is the mother and father, guilt from incestuous longings and
repressed aggression, in addition to social conditions. What is
sought is non-repression; the sexuality of infancy cannot be
found "out on the road" and we then hear:

I'm gonna write and tell mama for to please, ma'am, send
  for me. (x2)
Aw these women they don't treat me like I need to be.
  (Robert Hill, *I'm Going to Write and Tell Mother*)

Well, I left home for this woman and went into this world
   alone. (x2)
Now, I'm sorry, so sorry, that I ever left my home.
        (Leroy Carr, *Cruel Woman Blues*)

I'm gonna leave here walking, make home my second stop. (x2)
I'm gonna find my mother, she's the only friend I got.
        (Sonny Jones, *Won't Somebody Pacify My Mind*)

Leaving implies returning — what is sought is being left behind,
only to be sought again.

I'm leaving here, Mama don't you want to go. (x2)
Because I'm sick and tired of all this ice and snow.

When I get back to Memphis, you can bet I'll stay. (x2)
And I ain't gonna leave until that judgment day.

[*spoken*] Lord, if I just had railroad fare.

I wrote my gal a letter way down in Tennessee. (x2)
Told her I was up here hungry, hurry up and send for me.
        (Memphis Jug Band, *Goin' Back to Memphis*)

The ambivalence is inescapable:

I was thinking about going home, I don't believe that I will
   go. (x2)
I'm going to stay away a long time, oooh, well, well, like I
   did once before.

I try to be good every place I go. (x2)
But, now, you know, there will come a time, oooh, well,
   well, I will have some place, I know.

Now, if I go home, do you think that is the best place to
be? (x2)
Well, then again, if'n I go home, oooh, well, well, now, do
you think she will be mean to me?
(Peetie Wheatstraw, *Sweet Home Blues*)

The link between time and space is not lost in the blues. There
is a realization that what is sought for in space, from South to
North, must be sought for in time, from adulthood to childhood. At first, perhaps, the suspension of movement is our only
glimpse — after all, why travel if the goal is unattainable?

I can sit right here, think a thousand miles away.
(Memphis Jug Band, *Beale Street Mess Around*)

Then there is a vague comprehension that travelling is, after all,
a mental activity.

Well, the train has left the station with two lights on
behind. (x2)
Well, the blue light was my blues and the red light was my
mind.
(Robert Johnson, *Love in Vain*)

But the realization dawns fully and eloquently in *Long Ago Blues*
by Georgia Tom. Is deprivation being left or is childhood being
sought?

I didn't have no stocking,
I didn't have no shoes,
I didn't have no troubles,
And I didn't have no blues.
But that was long ago,
I mean it's long ago.
Now we usta have a good time,
Tell you that was long ago.

The blues singer has been cast as the wanderer; many of them did spend much of their lives on the road. While the blues singer has rarely, if ever, been the subject of psychoanalysis, the chronic wanderer has. Otto Fenichel (1945:370) says this: "The usual restlessness in the wanderers is rooted in the fact that for the most part the protection they seek once more becomes a danger, because the violence of their longing is felt as a dangerous instinct. To make comparative rest possible, the situation to which they are running must be near enough to the original unconscious goal to be acceptable as a substitute, and at the same time far enough removed not to create anxiety. When at home, the seaman thinks this place will be at sea; when aboard, at home."

This ambivalence, the dilemma of the sailor and the sea, is superbly exemplified by Uncle Bud Walker's classic line:

I want you to stand still, suitcase, till I find my clothes.
(Stand Up Suitcase Blues)

And this verse by Kokomo Arnold:

I'm scared to stay here, scared to leave this ol' bad luck
town. (x2)
But when I wake up every morning, my head is going
round and round.
(Bad Luck Blues)

We have seen that the songs reveal various levels and processes of mental functioning, various mechanisms of dealing with the conflictual disharmony of everyday life. Yet the songs themselves *are* mechanisms for dealing with despair, and while Freud has offered the term *sublimation* as descriptive of the mechanism whereby instinctual impulses become transformed into instincts with "social" (cultural) aims, the blues operates on a level which is at once creative (poetic) and revelatory (unalienated) of its

Jefferson County, Kentucky, 1920s.

instinctual sources. Not surprisingly, while acting themselves as
mechanisms for dealing with despair, the songs deal with other,
more conscious mechanisms for handling the despair that confronts the singer.

One of the favored mechanisms is flight (travel); fight, or
aggression, was inhibited through the fear of death or castration,
a fear which in the South was entirely reality-based, reactivated
from its infantile prototype, giving a peculiar sort of legitimacy
not only to Freud's theories, but to the white southerner's conception of the black as a child, with the whites as often the
simultaneously benevolent and hateful parents. Deprived of an
outlet for aggression by the whites' atrocious techniques of mastery (self-perpetuated by the whites by the internal inadequacy
of the technique and its constant need of reinforcement), the
black finds his aggression released on other blacks, or turned
inwards. Such is one source of despair, and, indeed, in a clinical
discussion of depression, David Rubinfine (1968:403) suggests,

"We may therefore infer that rage goes hand in hand with the experience of prolonged frustration, and that this rage, when it fails to elicit response, that is, to alter the environment, results in exhaustion and feelings of helplessness. Here then is the earliest experience of loss which results in the model for the genesis of depressive affect." This description of an infantile source of depression portrays vividly one of the psychological outcomes of black life in white America. Also, it portrays the inevitable fate of humanity at the mercy of modern civilization.

ALCOHOL AND DRUGS

> As long as we haven't been able to
> abolish a single cause of human
> desperation, we do not have the right to
> try to suppress the means by which man
> tries to clean himself of desperation.
> —Antonin Artaud

Drugs like heroin, alcohol, and marijuana are seized upon as weapons against the horrors of human existence, and as means for dealing with such conflicts, they are mentioned frequently in the blues.

You know I'm sitting 'round here drinking, just to help me to forget. (x2)
My baby left me this morning, I haven't found that woman yet.

Well, my baby left me this morning, she said, "James, I'm going away." (x2)
But I'm still sitting 'round here drinking, I ain't seen that girl today.
(Blind James Campbell, *Sitting Here Drinking*)

For the vast majority of the black working class, alcohol was far more popular, not to mention cheaper, than heroin. Even marijuana use must be considered minimal in comparison with alcohol consumption. Those who drank were often aware of the debilitating effects of alcohol, but the debilitating effect of civilization seemed more horrendous.

> [*spoken*] This is Tommy McClennan, the one who put out the *Whiskey Headed Woman* blues, instead of putting out the *Whiskey Headed Woman* blues I'm gonna put out "He's a whiskey headed man," just like myself and all the rest of you whiskey headed men.

> Now he's a whiskey headed man, and he stays drunk all the time. (x2)
> Now just as sure as he don't stop drinking, I believe he's going to lose his mind.

> Now every time I see this man, he's at some whiskey joint,
> Trying to catch a big bet so he can get another pint.
> 'Cause he's a whiskey headed man, etc.
> (Tommy McClennan, *Whiskey Head Man*)

As Blind Blake sang it:

> I went home last night, my baby won't let me in. (x2)
> She made me mad and I got in my gin.

> I've been drunk so long, dizzy all the time. (x2)
> Then I found out, whiskey ain't no friend to me.

> When I die, folks, without a doubt. (x2)
> You won't have to do nothing but pour me out.

I can't sleep and I can't eat a thing.(x2)
The woman I love has driv' me to drink.

I'm deep in a hole somebody else has dug. (x2)
Getting sick and tired of fighting that jug.
(Blind Blake, *Fighting The Jug*)

The last verse contains the implications of a partial disclaimer of responsibility, one which we can only echo.

In imagination as well as in reality, alcohol releases inhibitions and aggression, and is no doubt sought by many for that very reason.

The dealer ask me, "Peetie, how come you so rough?" (x2)
Well, now, I ain't bad, oooh well, well, but I just been
drinking that stuff.

That stuff will kill you, but it just won't quit. (x2)
It will get you to the place, oooh, well, well, that you don't
care who you hit.

I been drinking that stuff, and it went to my head. (x2)
It made me hit the baby in the cradle, oooh, well, well, and
kill my papa dead.

It made me hit the policeman, and knock him off his feet. (x2)
Taken his pistol and his star, oooh, well, well, and walking
up and down his beat.

I been drinking that stuff, I been drinking it all my days. (x2)
But the judge give me six months, oooh, well, well, to
change my drinking ways.
(Peetie Wheatstraw, *Drinking Man Blues*)

Franklin Street, Natchez, Mississippi, 1944.

For some, whiskey is the only thing that makes civilization bearable.

> Well, I drink so much whiskey till they call me whiskey
> man. (x2)
> Lord, I get drunk every morning with the whiskey bottle in
> my hand.
>
> Lord, my baby treats me mean, she keeps me worried all the
> time. (x2)

And if I didn't drink my whiskey, I believe I'd lose my
   mind.

When I drink whiskey, I don't mistreat my friends. (x2)
I am sober now, but I'm gonna get drunk again.

Lord, whiskey, whiskey, it don't mean me no good. (x2)
And I would stop drinking that whiskey, baby, if I only
   could.

Lord, lord, whiskey is killing me. (x2)
And why I can't stóp drinking whiskey, Lord, I just can't see.

My baby put me out, I'm just going from hand to hand.
   (x2)
And I drink so much whiskey till they call me whiskey
   man.
                (Black Bottom McPhail, *Whiskey Man Blues*)

The large number of references to alcohol in the blues, and
there are hundreds, throws into stark contrast the relatively
few mentions of other drugs: heroin, marijuana, and cocaine.
Heroin became illegal after 1914; marijuana, after 1937; alcohol
was illegal (with the passage of the Prohibition Act), although
plentiful and accessible, from 1920 through 1933 — the entire
range of the vintage blues recording years. It remains to be seen,
however, exactly how many blues artists were drawn to heroin,
marijuana, or cocaine. The statistics regarding drug use in general are usually those statistics circulated by the government and
are, consequently, quite biased, fraudulent, and valueless.
Regarding the blues singers, however, we have only a little more
to work with. Clarence Williams, jazz pianist, songwriter and
producer, has been quoted as saying, "But I never knew hardly
any musicians that took dope, it was mostly the girls. . ."! J. Mayo
Williams, one of the most prominent A & R men and talent

scouts for the blues recording industry, could only recall one incident involving any of his artists and marijuana, but it must be admitted that his administrative position might have precluded the establishment of any sort of intimacy during which drug use would be revealed. A small sampling of personal interviews indicates that marijuana was "around occasionally," mostly in association with jazz artists, and that heroin use among blues singers was relatively rare.

Nonetheless, the blues singer Champion Jack Dupree recorded three songs about heroin, each marked by his own sardonic humor. The first was *Junker Blues,* in 1941.

They call, they call me a junker 'cause I'm loaded all the
     time.
I don't need no reefers, I be knocked out with that angel
     wine.

Six months, six months ain't no sentence, and one year ain't
     no time.
They got boys in penitentiary doing from nine to ninety-
     nine.

I was standing, I was standing on the corner with my
     reefers in my hand.
Up step the sergeant, took my reefers out my hand.

My brother, my brother, used the needle and my sister
     sniffed cocaine.
I don't use no junk, I'm the nicest boy you ever seen.

My mother, my mother, she told me, and my father told me
     too.
That "That junk is a bad habit, why don't you leave it, too."

My sister, she even told me, and my grandma told me, too.

"That using junk, pardner, was gonna be the death of you."

His second version was called *Junker's Blues* (1958);

> [*spoken*] My, my, my. Sick as I can be.
>
> Some people call me a junker 'cause I'm loaded all the time.
> I just feel happy, and I feel good all the time.
>
> Some people say I use the needle and some say I sniff
> cocaine.
> But that's the best ol' feeling in the world I've ever seen.
>
> Say good-bye, good-bye to whiskey, Lord, and so long to
> gin.
> I just want my reefers, I just want to feel high again.
>
> [*spoken*] Oh, yes, I'm a junker. I feel all right.
>
> Some people, some people crave for chicken and some
> crave for porterhouse steak.
> But when I get loaded, Lord, I want my milk and cake.
>
> [*spoken*] Oh, yeah. That's all I want now. They call me a
> junker 'cause I'm loaded all the time. But that ain't nothing
> if I feel good all the time.

At the same 1958 session, Dupree recorded *Can't Kick the Habit*. More sombre than the first two, the pessimistic mood of this song is shattered by Dupree's remarkable candor in the last line.

> Well, I can't kick this habit, and this junk is killing me. (x2)
> Ever since I started this habit, everything's been down on me.
>
> I hung around my friends and smoked reefers, and I

thought I was doing all right. (x2)
Now I've lost a good woman, and I have no place to sleep
at night.

Well, I went to the doctor, see could he cure this habit for
me. (x2)
He looked at me and shook his head and said that dope is
killing me.

[*spoken*] Yes, I know it's killing me. But I feel good anyhow.
I wish I had listened to what my mother said. She told me
that dope wasn't no good. I didn't pay it no mind. I
thought I was doing (all right). Now I'm just as sick as I
can be.

It don't pay nobody just to live their life so fast. (x2)
If you just take it slow and easy, just as long as this habit lasts.

Dupree's songs are remarkable for the striking portrayal of the
ambivalence in the addict — a conflict which is itself relieved
by each shot. Dupree suggests that the lot of the addict is not an
entirely miserable one, while the following song, *Knocking
Myself Out*, implies that misery precedes drug use, in this case
marijuana, the drug being resorted to when other defense
mechanisms fail.

Listen girls and boys, I've got one stick.
Give me a match and let me take a whiff quick.
I'm gonna knock myself out; I'm gonna kill myself.
I'm gonna knock myself out, gradually, by degrees.

I started blowing my gage, and I was having my fun,
Spied the police and I started to run.
I was knocking myself out, etc.

But the very moment I looked around,
(My) mind said "Yack, throw that gage on the ground."
The policeman said, "Just kill yourself."
The policeman said, "Just kill yourself."
He said, "Knock yourself out, Yack, gradually, by degrees."

I used to didn't blow gage, did nothing of the kind,
But my man quit me and I changed my mind.
That's why I'm knocking myself out, etc.

I'm gonna blow this jive, it's a sin and a shame,
But it's the only thing that ease my heart off of my man.
When I knock myself out, when I kill myself.
I just knock myself smack out, gradually, by degrees.
  (Yack Taylor, *Knocking Myself Out*)

Marijuana was also the theme of one of the more popular blues,
If You're a Viper.

Dreamed about a reefer five feet long, mighty mezz, but not
  too strong,
You'll be high, but not for long, if you're a viper.

I'm the queen of everything, I've got to be high before I
  can swing.
Light a tea and let it be, if you're a viper.

When your throat gets dry, you know you're high,
  everything is dandy.
Truck on down to the candy store, bust your conk on
  peppermint candy.

Then you'll know your body's sent, you don't care if you
don't pay rent.
The sky is high and so am I, if you're a viper.
(Rosetta Howard and the Harlem Hamfats,
If You're a Viper)

That drugs provide escape from the misery of life, there is no
doubt. But there is indeed another dimension to drug use,
hinted at by Preble and Casey (1969:22): "Given the social conditions of the slums and their effects on family and individual
development, the odds are strongly against the development of
a legitimate, non-deviant career that is challenging and reward-
ing . . . If anyone can be called passive in the slums, it is not the
heroin user, but the one who submits to and accepts these conditions." Indeed, there is much more to be said — notwithstanding the simplistic vulgarism that heroin is merely a
capitalist plot to enslave the minds of the proletariat — for
Preble and Casey's observation, coupled with what we have seen
in the songs, suggests the rediscovery of the poetic dimension of
drug use as a revolt against everyday degradation. By refusing to
accept the enslavement imposed by bourgeois society, the drug
user expresses a specific form of negation, the negation of
despair, and the definite (but hardly definitive!) negation of
bourgeois civilization as a whole.

Let us recall here the use of narcotics by a long tradition of
poets — from Coleridge and Poe to Francis Thompson and
Harry Crosby, from Baudelaire and Gautier to Roger Gilbert-
Lecomte and Antonin Artaud. From the poetic standpoint, drug
use in and of itself is of comparatively minor interest — far
more significant is the specific use made of drugs by poetic
explorers in provoking *inspiration*. Some poetic thinkers, in fact,
have utilized their drug experiences as points of departure for
elaborate philosophical investigations. Thomas De Quincey, for
example, avowed that he wrote his *Confessions of an English
Opium-Eater* to reveal "the power that belongs potentially to

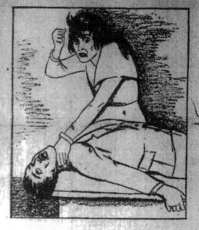

dreams." And the American Benjamin Paul Blood, following years of extensive use of nitrous oxide, ether and other substances, tirelessly defended his conception of the "anaesthetic revelation," founded on the principle that "naked life is realized only outside of sanity altogether." Here as elsewhere inspiration retains its centrality in human experience.

It is only the academics, then, who will wonder (or care) whether Victoria Spivey really used cocaine or not when she made *Dope Head Blues*. For it is in this song that we find the convulsive liberation of the image that so closely links the blues to the boldest efforts of modern poetry: the images of desire, at once of the unconscious as well as the conscious, set free:

Just give me one more sniffle, another sniffle of that dope. (x2)
I'll catch a cow like a cowboy, throw a bull without a rope.

Doggone, I got more money than Henry Ford or John D.
   ever had. (x2)
I bit a dog last Monday, and 40 doggone dogs went mad.

I feel like a fighting rooster, feeling better than I ever felt. (x2)
(I could have) pneumonia, and still I feel I've got the best
   health.

Say, Sam, go get my airplane and drive it up to my door. (x2)
I think I'll fly to London, these monkey men make mama
   sore.

The President sent for me, the Prince of Wales is on my
   trail. (x2)
They worry me so much, I'll take another sniff and put
   them both in jail.

MALE SUPREMACY

> There are no limits to masculine egotism
> in ordinary life. In order to change the
> conditions of life we must learn to see
> them through the eyes of women.
> —Leon Trotsky

Anyone who has listened to blues for even the shortest time cannot fail to note that a large number of the male singers' references to women are overtly demeaning or deprecatory.[8]

I don't want no woman, can't cheat neither rob and steal. (x2)
I'd rather see her working out in some farmer's field.
  (Julius Daniels, *Richmond Blues*)

Plain looking women live out in the country 'cause folks
  just don't want 'em 'round. (x2)
When you find an ugly woman living in Harlem, she's
  either rich or from some other town.
  (Dr. Clayton, *Angels in Harlem*)

In an earlier work (1971), I suggested that Peetie Wheatstraw, was, at least in his lyrics, rather typical in his masculine egotism. His lyrics reveal that he regarded women as potential "mistreaters," and indeed, only a few of his more than one hundred and fifty songs regard women wholly favorably.

What makes me love my baby? She loved me when I was
  down. (x2)
Well, now, she was nice and kind, oooh, well, well, she did
  not dog me around.

You know the most of the women listen to what people
  say. (x2)

Well, but now, you know, my babe, oooh, well, well, she's
just the other way.

Well, now, she give me money and kept me nice and clean. (x2)
Well, now, you know, when I was down, oooh, well, well,
my babe didn't treat me mean.

Now I'm good to my baby since I'm up on my feet. (x2)
Well, now, I don't care, oooh, well, well, if I never see a
woman on the street.
(Peetie Wheatstraw, *Good Woman Blues*)

Even in this affectionate song, he depicts the relationship as
exploitative, but there is no indication that Wheatstraw was
actually an exploiter in this sense. The songs may reflect only his
desire to maintain such relationships. He may have failed utterly,
he may never have tried; we cannot know. And we don't care. It
is not our objective here to analyze individuals through a study
of the manifest content of the lyrics. The tendency to demean
women that we see in the blues relates to numerous aspects of
black family life, and in general, to the familial patterns of modern civilization. The resultant ambivalence is strikingly por-
trayed in the blues. The aggression, hostility, and their typical
elaborations (deprecation, discrimination) which might ordinar-
ily be subject to repression are given free rein:

Now, the blues don't mean
  nothing when you got your
  six-shooter on your side. (x2)
If your women mistreats you,
  shoot her and grab a train and
  ride.
    (Georgia Tom, *Six-Shooter
    Blues*)

Or Wheatstraw, again, with *Peetie Wheatstraw Stomp No. 2:*

> Everybody hollering "Here come that Peetie Wheatstraw." (x2)
> Now he's better known by the Devil's Son-in-Law.
>
> Everybody wondering what that Peetie Wheatstraw do. (x2)
> 'Cause every time you hear him, he's coming out with
> something new.
>
> He makes some happy, some he makes cry. (x2)
> Well, now, he made one old lady go hang herself and die.
>
> This is Peetie Wheatstraw, I'm always on the line. (x2)
> Save up your nickels and dimes, you can come up to see me
> sometime.

And again:

> I used to have a woman that lived up on the hill. (x2)
> She was crazy about me, oooh, well, well, because I worked
> at the Chicago mill.
>
> You can hear the woman hollering when the Chicago mill
> whistle blow. (x2)
> Cryin' "A-Loose my man, oooh, well, well, please, and let
> him go."
>
> If you want a-plenty women, boys, work at the Chicago
> mill. (x2)
> You don't have to give them nothing, oooh, well, well, just
> tell them that you will.
>
> When I went to work, I worked at the Chicago mill. (x2)
> So I could get plenty women, oooh, well, well, at my free
> good will.

So, bye bye, boys, go on and have your thrill. (x2)
You don't need no money, oooh, well, well, just say you
   work at the Chicago mill.
>   (Peetie Wheatstraw, *Chicago Mill Blues*)

A relatively sophisticated songwriter, Leadbelly composed *National Defense Blues* when defense contracts during World War II made many jobs available to women that were formerly held by men.

I had a little woman working on the National Defense. (x2)
That woman got to the place act like she did not have no
   sense.

Just because she was working, making so much dough. (x2)
That woman got to the place, she did not love me no more.

Every pay-day would come, her check was big as mine. (x2)
That woman thought that Defense was gonna last all the
   time.

That Defense is gone, just listen to my song. (x2)
Since that Defense is gone that woman done lose her home.

I will tell you the truth, and it's got to be the fact. (x2)
Since that Defense been gone that woman lose her
   Cadillac.

Mercy Dee, one of the most eloquent and articulate of the bluesmen, sang these words in *Pity and a Shame.*

Now it's a pity and a shame, the tricky actions of a woman's
   brain. (x2)
Soon as she find you want her and her only, right away she
   go and make a change.

Now a woman will fight, kill, and struggle, trying to hold a
    man. (x2)
But when the competition is over, right away she go and
    make a change.

I know you can't case a woman, but there's one habit it
    would be wise to form. (x2)
Be sure she's yours and yours only when you got her lying
    up in your arms.

Now it's a pity and a shame that a woman will never see
    the light. (x2)
She'll go out of her way to pull something that'll make her
    suffer the rest of her life.

The implication that much of the content of affective relationships is subject to repression in more alienated sectors of society
suggests that what operates relatively freely in the blues in the
form of male supremacy and domination is analogous if not
identical to what operates more secretly in other relations
among those more alienated and repressed. What is latent but
nonetheless operative and effective in many of us is manifest in
the blues. It would be a mistake, as I have pointed out earlier, to
label the blues singer as non-repressed, for repression certainly
contributes to the creation of the patterns we are studying. But
the creative process affects the mental structure in specific ways,
and in the blues in a rather unique way, so that we are presented
with material that would not be apparent if we were investigating a number of other creative activities.

The most obvious characteristic of the blues singer's male
chauvinism is that it is bound inseparably to the repressive civilization that fostered it. The unusual economic, political, and
cultural discrimination to which the blacks have been subjected
enables male supremacy to present itself within a unique framework in the blues, but male chauvinism is hardly an exclusive

property of the black working class; it is found at all levels of society and is symptomatic of a large number of afflictions that currently inhibit us, not the least of which is the stifling atmosphere of civilized family life.

LIBERATION OF WOMEN

> The change in a historical epoch can always be determined by the progress of women toward freedom ... The degree of emancipation of women is the natural measure of general emancipation.
> — Charles Fourier

Not at all divorced from this is the fact that implicit in the songs of the women blues singers is the demand for an abandonment of male supremacy, and the broader demand for an end to the repressive aspects of modern civilization as a whole. In spite of this, little if any attention has been given to the blues in the various periodicals devoted to women's liberation, although there seems to be an ever-growing number of white female blues enthusiasts, many of whom voice a strong preference for women blues singers. Undeniably, there is a strong element of identification in the refusal to accept further degradation.

You done cause me to weep, baby, now, swear you done
cause me to moan. (x2)
Well, you know by that, rider, I ain't gonna be here long.
(Louise Johnson, *All Night Long Blues*)

Or, as Mississippi Matilda sang:

Now, I'm a hard working woman, I work hard all the time. (x2)
But it seems like my baby, he isn't satisfied.

I have to go to my work, baby, 'tween midnight and day,

I didn't think my baby would treat me this away.
(repeat both lines)

Now I'm a hard working woman, Lord, I'm becoming a
   rolling stone. (x2)
And the way my baby treats me, I ain't gonna be here long.

Now do you remember the morning, baby, you knocked on
   my door,
You told me, daddy, you didn't have nowhere to go.
(repeat both lines)

Now I'm a hard working woman, babe, (I work hard, sick
   or well?) (x2)
But I can't stand my baby, huh, he is a heap of hell.
            (Mississippi Matilda, *Hard Working Woman*)

We have already quoted Merline Johnson's *Reckless Life Blues,*
and while there are a number of songs that similarly demand an
end to repression, one of the most specifically revealing is this
one by Ida Cox:

You never get nothing by being an angel child,
You better change your ways and get real wild.
'Cause wild women don't worry, wild women don't have
   the blues.
          (Ida Cox, *Wild Women Don't Have the Blues*)

The songs of the women blues singers are, in a number of ways,
similar to the songs of the men. The same themes predominate,
and alongside the vivid portrayals of humiliation and the stark
aggressiveness, there are numerous open declarations of erotic
desire, as in Bessie Smith's *Empty Bed Blues,* or as in these lines
by Memphis Minnie:

If you see my rooster, please run him on back home. (x2)
I haven't found no eggs in my basket, ooowee, since my
  rooster been gone.
          (*If You See My Rooster*)

Or these:

They call me oven, they say that I'm red hot. (x2)
They say I got something the other gals ain't got.
          (Nellie Florence, *Jacksonville Blues*)

I need a plenty grease in my frying pan
'Cause I don't want my meat to burn.
          (Mandy Lee [Elizabeth Smith], *I Need a Plenty
          of Grease in My Frying Pan*)

Ain't but the one thing that makes me sore,
When you grind me one time and just won't do it no more.
          (Dorothea Trowbridge and Stump Johnson,
          Steady Grinding)

As in the last verse, we often find that coupled with the desire is
its frustration.

Hello there, Central, please give me my best man. (x2)
Well, I gave you the right number, gee, I can't understand.

Moaning, groaning, groaning, phoning, oooh, there must be
  somebody there.
Central, Central, tell me what's that I hear.

Lord, could it be another woman there? (x2)
So tired of walking the floor, wringing my hands, and
  pulling my hair.

SPIVEY, VICTORIA
Blood Hound Blues
Dirty T. B. Blues
Moaning the Blues
New York Blues
Showered with Blues
Telephoning the Blues

Waiting, watching, praying, dreaming, oooh, Central, won't
   you let me know?
'Cause I can get a daddy most any place I go.

Aw, Central, Central, I've been telephoning the blues,
Central, Central, please give me good news.
I've been phoning, phoning, I've been telephoning all night
   long.
Bet you fifty to one hundred something's going on wrong.
      (Victoria Spivey, *Telephoning the Blues*)

Now look here, Daddy, see what you have done; (x2)
You done caused me to love you, now your other woman's
   come.

Lordy, lordy, lordy, look what trouble I've seen. (x2)
50,000 other gals taking my man from me.
      (Sara Martin, *A Green Gal Can't Catch On*)

Our own emotional lives, like the lives of the singers themselves,
are often victimized by confusion — specific psychic mechanisms (repression, isolation) often give rise to feelings of vague
discomfort and anxiety which elude a more specific elaboration.
Often we just "have the blues."

Now you talk about the black snake blues,
Well, you haven't heard no moaning yet.
Awww, moaning, all day long.
And when you hear this moaning, it's moaning you will
   never forget.

Ahhaaah, ahhaww, ummmhmmm, ahhhooooh.
Well, I know I can moan, I don't see how I lost my happy
   home.

Well it was on a Sunday morning, I didn't feel so good.
I felt like a cow when she had lost her cud.
I begin my moaning, all day long.
And when you hear me a-moaning, you can bet sweet
    mama feels good.

Ahhh oooh, ahh, ooh, ummmhmmm, aaah oooh.
Lord, I know I can moan, I don't see how I lost my home.

Well if I'm the only one in my family to take a biscuit to
    pieces,
Put it back just like it was.
Aw, with my moaning, all day long
Yes, I can kick my leg high, and you oughta see me do the
    buck (bug?).
                    (Victoria Spivey, *Moaning The Blues*)

In regard to instinctual repression and its fate, the woman blues
singer functions in a manner similar to the male blues singer.
But in addition to this, the woman blues singer exemplifies the
specific fate of woman at the hands of a society ruled by the
white male bourgeoisie, wherein the female is subject to a
seemingly endless variety of forms of subjugation. This subjugation, as we have seen to some extent, is reflected in her songs.
One of the most characteristic degradations of the lower class
black woman is her frequent necessity to resort to prostitution,
either as a means of economic sustenance or as a method of ful-
filling the expectations (and exploitations) of her male partner
or pimp.

Times done got hard, money's done got scarce,
Stealing and robbing is going to take place.
'Cause tricks ain't walking, tricks ain't walking no more. (x2)
And I'm going to rob somebody if I don't make me some
    dough.

I'm going to do just like a blind man, stand and beg for change.
And tell these 'resting officers, "change my tricking name."
'Cause tricks ain't walking, tricks ain't walking no more. (x2)
And I've got to make my living, don't care where I go.

I'm going to learn these walking tricks what it's all about.
I'm going to get them in my house and ain't going to let them out.
'Cause tricks ain't walking, tricks ain't walking no more. (x2)
And I can't make no money, don't care where I go.

I got up this moring with the rising sun,
Been walking all day and I ain't caught a one.
'Cause tricks ain't walking, tricks ain't walking no more. (x2)
And I can't make a dime, don't care where I go.
        (Bessie Jackson, *Tricks Ain't Walking No More*)

I stood on the corner all night long counting the stars one by one. (x2)
I didn't make me no money, Bob, and I can't go back home.

My man sets in the window with his .45 in his hand. (x2)
Every now and then he gets to hollering at me and tells me, "You'd better not miss that man."
        [*spoken*] I've got him baby.

My daddy ain't got no shoes, Bob, now it done got cold. (x2)
I'm gonna grab me somebody if I don't make myself some dough.

I'm going to the (quarter-bowl?), see what I can find. (x2)
And if I make a hundred dollars, I'm gonna bring my daddy ninety-nine
        (Memphis Minnie, *Hustlin' Woman Blues*)

As Lil Johnson sang it:

> Scufflin' done got so hard until I can't hardly eat. (x2)
> Everywhere I turn, baby, the police is on my beat.
> (Lil Johnson, *Scuffling Woman Blues*)

If there is implicit in the blues a "feminist" critique of society, linked to this is a broader critique of repressive civilization, based not on any sex-specificity, nor even on the peculiar position of the black in American culture, although this characteristic is the major force from which blues draws its unique perspective as well as its specific form; the basis of the critique is the general level of degradation of human life throughout the world at the present time.

NIGHT

> The pearl of the dragon is the splendor
> of the night, night from the beginning the
> foremost declaration of the sun's freedom.
> — Philip Lamantia

The nature of the poetic terrain covered by the blues suggests that in the minds of the performers as well as in the minds of the audience, the blues is a music closely associated with ideas concerning the night. This is yet another aspect that unites the blues to the most modern and uncompromising efforts on the poetic plane. Surrealism has inherited, extended and systematized the nocturnal presence manifest in such pre-Romantic and Romantic works as Edward Young's *Night-Thoughts*, William Blake's *Vata, or the Four Zoas (A Dream in Nine Nights)*, Novalis' *Hymns to the Night*, etc. It is thus entirely natural that surrealism and the blues should meet here on common ground, for this shared nocturnal sensibility sets them both apart from the dominant literary fashions of this century (as exemplified, for example, by such strictly *diurnal* "poets" as T. S. Eliot, Ezra Pound, or Robert Frost.[9]

The axis around which this whole subject revolves is love, but there is a network of concepts associated with loneliness, fear, desertion, and rejection, which not only are associated in our minds with the idea of night but are also the subject of numerous blues. Other blues songs, also about the night, are woven from a more harmonious fabric and deal directly with the positive aspects of love, all perhaps inspired by the fact that for most of us the day is devoted to work and the night is available for play (love). Typical of these songs is Roosevelt Sykes's *Night Time is the Right Time* ("... to be with the one you love"). But more frequently we hear songs such as these:

In the wee midnight hours, long 'fore the break of day. (x2)
When the blues creep up on you and carry your mind away.

While I lay in my bed and cannot go to sleep. (x2)
While my heart's in trouble and my mind is thinking deep.

My mind is running back to days of long ago. (x2)
And the one I love, I don't see her anymore.
    (Leroy Carr, *Midnight Hour Blues*)

Got the blues before sunrise, tears standing in my eyes. (x2)
It's such a miserable feeling, a feeling I do despise.
    (Leroy Carr, *Blues Before Sunrise*)

Your darkest hour is just 'fore day,
That's when your sorrow will vanish away.
    (Tampa Red, *Travel On*)

During the two-day recording session during which Leroy Carr made *Midnight Hour Blues* (above), he also recorded the following titles: *How Long Has That Evening Train Been Gone?*, *Quittin' Papa*, *Lonesome Nights*, *I Keep the Blues*, *Gone Mother Blues*, *Moonlight Blues* and *The Depression Blues!* There are numerous references in the blues regarding that particular form of despair so closely associated with the night, and it is only after resigning oneself not to dwell on the more superficial aspects of the night that we begin to appreciate the unconscious factors that contribute to our conception of the night and its unique qualities. The blues are articulate in terms of description and association, but a more elaborate explanation will not carry us far from our subject.

The night has always been the time that we most regularly engage in sleeping and dreaming. At night, our desires and needs have found expression (often distorted by the dream), and at night we have regularly faced our fear and horror of these same desires (or perhaps our fear of punishment for these desires). At night, too, we have most ardently confirmed the possibilities of our lives, projecting our wishes into dreams, myths, poetry, and of course, song. The blues is indeed of the night, regardless of the immense contribution made by the incidents of daily living, and regardless of when, day or night, the blues is played. I think that any of our emotional states can be traced back to their moments of greatest intensity *at night* — through the dream and through the vicissitudes of our own infantile sexuality, fear, and aggression, but primarily through the dream. Surely it is not rare or at all infrequent for "traumatic" incidents to befall the infant during the day, but I feel that except in unusual cases, even daylight events do not secure their decisiveness without the characteristic effects and elaborations of the night and the dream.

Given this, and given the almost universal confidence placed in the sunrise:

The big star falling, mama, 'tain't long 'fore day. (x2)
Maybe this sunshine will drive these blues away.
            (Blind Willie McTell, *Mama, 'Tain't Long Fo' Day*)

we are required to comment not only on the dawn but again on creative activity, as specifically manifested in the blues.

While we are all familiar with the possibilities of the horrors of the night, and while we may be willing to exploit these horrors until they fade into revelation, we must admit that perhaps the most despairing phenomenon of all is the *dawn of horror,* that feeling of isolation and melancholy so characteristic of night that solidifies rather than dissolves at daybreak. Against this we have few weapons; the proverbial "promise of the dawn" having been broken, there is very little that one can do. But what is significant is that this moment of despair (at the dawn) does not call forth the blues, in the musical sense. Often only tears or a waking glass of whiskey can appear at first, and it would be a mistake to think that the blues replaces tears. Those who think that while one man or woman mourns, the blues singer plays (or sings) are mistaken. Not all levels of despair can be mastered by singing. Once again we come across the necessity for the "aesthetic disguise," for a certain distance is necessary before despair can be transformed into a blues. The most painful states of humanity cannot find their way into song until some *distance* in time, space, language, or structure is placed between the experience and the performer.

But the blues, even those blues that deal manifestly with the subject of night, cannot be depicted simply as a music of despair. It would be just as much an error of emphasis to depict the blues as a music of pure joy; but while our present condition in modern civilization fosters despair in most of our activities, the blues nonetheless express a full range of emotional and imaginative possibilities:

Hurry down sunshine, see what tomorrow bring. (x2)
May bring drops of sorrow, and it may bring drops of rain.
    (Leroy Carr, *Hurry Down Sunshine*)

Sun going down, dark gon' catch me here.
    (Robert Johnson, *Crossroads Blues*)

All in my sleep, I can hear my doorbell ring. (x2)
When I turned my light on, Lord, there wasn't a doggone
thing.

(Smokey Hogg, *Dark Clouds*)

Psychoanalytic investigations have revealed that in the unconscious blacks are (to whites) often identified not only with
fathers and siblings (Sterba 1945) but with a number of ideas
associated with anality (Kovel 1970). The observations of
Ferenczi (1914) and Freud (1908) on the associations between
anality and money only hint at the huge network of unconscious associations involving blacks, blackness, money, evil, anality, the night, and of course, the blues. As far as I know, a number
of the above associative paths remain uninvestigated, and the few
psychoanalytic investigations that have been carried out (Sterba,
Kovel, Rodgers 1960) do more to reveal the dynamic mental
processes that mould prejudice and underlie discriminatory
practices than they do to reveal even slightly the secrets of the
night, much less the essence of enchantment in the blues.

ANIMALS

Many have written on beasts without
sufficiently investigating their moral
resemblance to man from the point of
view of passional analogy . . . Poets alone
seem to have understood the true
character of the beast.
—Alphonse Toussenel

The number of blues lyrics concerning animals is enormous,
and this predilection for animal images is another indication of
the specific poetic fertility of the blues. In a brief essay on Aloys
Zötl, the 19th-century "naive" artist who painted only unusual
animals in unusual settings, André Breton (1956:355) noted that

"the animal kingdom. . . remains such an enigmatic aspect in each of our lives and. . . plays such an essential role in the symbolism of the unconscious mind." Blues lyrics permit us to see with what seductive facility animal images may be used for poetical redefinition of human relationships, while at the same time, in extending essentially "totemic" frames of reference into everyday life, they challenge all limited "humanist" conceptions of man's "righteousness." For animals provide an irrational stumbling-block for humanist-rationalist no less than for religious ideology. And just as repressive terminology employs animal terms to *denounce* truly human behavior — as when a schoolteacher tells children at play to "stop acting like animals" — so the blues singers' *celebration* of truly human behavior (especially sexual love) in animal terms is an especially striking example of the *distance* separating the blues from the dominant ideology.

This is from Big Joe Williams' *Shetland Pony Blues,* derived from Charlie Patton's versions of the same song:

Hitch up my pony, saddle up my black mare. (x2)
I got a brownskin woman, baby, in this world somewhere.

While Casey Bill sang these lines in his *Long-Eared Mule:*

Well, my baby left me this morning, and we was chilly and
    cool. (x2)
Couldn't find nothing to ride and catch my baby, ooh, well,
    well, I had to saddle up my long-eared mule.

Well, well, I seen my baby running, I knowed she was
    leaving town. (x2)
I had to ride my long-eared mule, ooh, well, to run my
    baby down.

Well, well, I wanted to catch my baby, beg her please not to
    go. (x2)

A "long-eared mule" picks up filled cotton sacks: Mississippi Delta, September 1947.

But that doggone mule taken sick, ooowee, that mule
    couldn't run no more.

Well, well, my baby caught that train, she left me that long-
    eared mule to ride. (x2)
When that train left the station, ooh, well, well, that mule
    taken the blues and died.

Sonny Boy Williamson's *Ground Hog Blues* is a magnificent composition:

Well, I'm that walking ground-hog, Mama, I walks around
    in my den. (x2)

Lord, if I come out and see my shadow, darling, I believe I'll
   go back in.

Lord, I want to hear some swinging music,
I want to hear Fats Waller's sound,
If I get to jitterbugging,
I can get my hole down in the ground,
'Cause I'm that walking ground-hog,
Man, and I walks around in my den.
Now, if I come out and see my shadow and my mama don't
   love me,
I believe I'll go back in.

Now and I need some petting, baby,
Baby, you know what I mean.
Now, if you don't pet me, baby,
I believe I'll go back down in New Orleans,
Because I'm that walking ground-hog, etc.

Many more examples could be quoted; the ones that immediately follow deal mostly with spiders and insects.

Detail from a 1928 Bessie Smith ad.

122

I wake up every night around midnight, peoples, I just can't
sleep no more. (x2)
Only crickets and frogs to keep me company and the wind
howling around my door.
(Mercy Dee, *One Room Country Shack*)

Saw a big black spider creeping up my bedroom wall. (x2)
Found he was only going to get his ashes hauled.
(Sylvester Weaver, *Black Spider Blues*)

Well, let me be your black spider, build my web up beside
your wall. (x2)
Well, I'll build it so good, mama, ooh, well, well, you won't
want to get it down at all.

Well, if you let me be your spider, I'll be the sweetest man
in town. (x2)
Well, I'll bet my bottom dollar, baby, ooh, well, well, you
can look up as long as I look down.
(Johnny Shines, *Black Spider Blues*)

A curious and prominent position in the popular mythology of
the South must be reserved for the boll weevil. Arriving from
Mexico, this bug with a long snout is one of the most notorious pests in American history: it devoured vast acres of cotton,
which, prior to World War I, was the staple of the Southern
economy. In one decade boll weevils were responsible for the
destruction of some 25,000,000 bales of cotton, nearly a sixth of
the crop. Efforts to exterminate it failed. Desperate farmers, to
avert bankruptcy, turned to other crops and discovered, to their
astonishment, that sugar cane, potatoes, corn and peanuts
yielded better profits than had cotton. The tiny boll weevil,
then, was the instigator of a far-reaching agricultural revolution:
the overthrow of the one-crop economy. It is thus less bizarre
than might seem at first sight that in the cotton-belt town of
Enterprise, Alabama, there is a public monument of a female

When the boll weevil overthrew the cotton economy, many families like this one began raising peanuts. Louisiana, 1948.

human figure holding aloft a replica of the insect, bearing this inscription: "In profound appreciation of the boll weevil and what it has done as the herald of prosperity."

In the blues, however, we find that the boll weevil is often the bearer of very different tidings.

> Hey, boll weevil, don't sing them blues no more. (x2)
> Boll weevil's here, boll weevil's everywhere you go.
> (Bessie Smith, *Boweavil Blues*)

This is another version, by Leadbelly:

> First time I seen the boll weevil, he was sitting on a square.
> Next time I seen a boll weevil, he had his whole family there.
> He's a looking for a home. He's a looking for a home.

The old lady said to the old man, "I've been trying my level
best,
Keep these boll weevils out of my brand new cotton dress.
It's full of holes. And it's full of holes."

The old man said to the old lady, "What do you think of that?
I got one of the boll weevils out of my brand new Stetson hat,
And it's full of holes. And it's full of holes."

Now the farmer said to the merchant, "I never made but
one bale.
Before I let you have that last one, I will suffer and die in jail.
And I will have a home. And I will have a home."

That the boll weevil tale is one of persistance (and not simply pes-
tilence) is supported by the "I will have a home" refrain in the last
verse, sung by the farmer to the merchant, *signifying* by means of
identification on the boll weevil's refrain, "He's looking for a home."

Detail from a 1927/8 ad.

In the cases of several blues singers the "totemic" significations are so marked that they have adopted animals as nicknames or professional names: Howlin' Wolf, Hound Dog Taylor, Bumble Bee Slim, Bo Weavil Jackson, etc. Victoria Spivey's *Black Snake Blues* brought her such renown that to this day her album jackets are emblazoned with a pen-and-ink portrait of her draped with a large snake.

Of course there are numerous folk references to animals in blues; that is, references drawn from traditional lore, minstrel songs, Aesop's *Fables* and African tales. It is true, too, that references to the most ordinary animals — creatures of barnyard and woodland — predominate. Even "traditional" and "common" lines, however, often seem fresh and brilliant in contrast to the insipid trivia of most "popular" songs: for example, "make a rabbit hug a hound." But there are some blues-songs in which the animal imagery rises to a unique level of humor and fantasy, as in this tantalizing fairy tale by Victoria Spivey:

Folks, I'm telling you something that I saw with my own
  eyes,
As I passed the pond one day.
The old alligator was teaching his babies to do the Georgia
  Grind,
And I heard one of them say,
This is a social, but the alligators' pond's going dry.
Yeah, it is a social but alligators' pond's going dry.
Now old Mr. Alligator, he got way back,
He said, "Look out, children, I'm (throwing water off my?)
  back."
Aww, it was a social, but the alligators' pond went dry.

Aww, it must have been a social for the alligators' pond
  went dry.
Aww, it must have been a social for the alligators' pond to
  go dry.

Victoria Spivey, Walter Horton and a "mean black snake."

Now old Mr. Alligator, he got real hot.
He said, "We're gonna have the function whether there's
  water or not."
Aww, it was a social but alligators' pond went dry.
Well, if you don't believe what I'm saying, ask old alligator
  Jack.
Wasn't a drop of water in the pond when he got back.
It was a social, but the alligators' pond went dry.
  (*The Alligator Pond Went Dry*)

Blues Nectar (1975) by Ronald L. Papp.

WORK

> There is no use being alive if one must
> work. The event from which each of us is
> entitled to expect the revelation of his
> own life's meaning *is not earned by work*.
> — André Breton

Viewing the blues as the poetry and music of the black working class, we cannot help but be intrigued by the blues singers' treatment of the theme of work — alienated labor, and toil. If we recall that it is the *purpose* and not the *content* of the act that determines whether or not it is actually work, we find that the specific activity of blues singing occupies a peculiar position on the scale. We have already emphasized that the blues is a relatively unalienated creative activity, but more must be clarified. Certainly blues singing offers the singer much gratification and relaxation (at times), and while it might often appear as a form of play, it is just as often *work*.

On 22 November 1939 Tommy McClennan recorded eight songs for the Bluebird label. We have no way of knowing how many false starts, re-takes, or mistakes contributed to the lengthening of the session, but perhaps it was gruelling, for the last recorded song of the day begins with this spoken "aside" from McClennan:

(Now get on this here.) This is the last one you got now;
When you play these blues, you ain't got to play no more.

Of course, for anyone who has ever been in a studio during a blues recording session, it need hardly be said that work (as well as play) is involved. But the blues retains its capacity to reflect desire, and these lines by Peetie Wheatstraw, in the light of the explanation following them, indicate that the blues singer regards, or would like to regard, blues singing as play and not work.

I got a woman take care of me, yes, she's just only sweet
sixteen. (x2)
I never done a day's work in my life, ooh, well, well, I don't
know even what work means.

Now work was made for two things, that was a fool and a
mule. (x2)
I wouldn't start to work, ooh, well, well, because I didn't go
to school.
(Confidence Man)

The above lyric was "explained" by a friend of Wheatstraw's,
Teddy Darby: "Peetie never did have a regular job 'cause he
never needed one; he just always played around somewhere, just
playing and singin,' and I never known him to have a job"
(Garon 1971:92).

While a number of musicians consider their musical activity
per se to be something less than work, many rely on their musical ability as a means of economic sustenance, work. The slang
term *work,* aside from its other meanings, is often introduced to
describe a musical performance that, in terms of *labor,* exceeds
normal expectations, when a musician becomes heatedly and
intensely involved in a performance and when certain aspects of
relaxation and effortlessness seem to disappear. And while it is
no accident that musical instruments, unlike machines, are said
to be *played,* it would be insulting to suggest that those blues
singers who play the blues for their living do not really work.
The term *play* merely hints at the nature of the satisfaction and
libidinal gratification that is available to the blues musicians,
however hard they work, a gratification that is not necessarily
available in other sorts of work.[10]

Of course, a large number of blues artists are forced (like most
of us) to hold jobs other than musical ones. The blues reflects
not only the conditions under which the black workers do their

Black workers at furnace company, 1928.

work, but the attitudes of the workers as well, urban and industrial, rural and agricultural.

> I got a job in a steel mill,
> Trucking steel like a slave,
> Five long years, every Friday
> I went straight home with all my pay.
> (Eddie Boyd, *Five Long Years*)

Hear that bell ringing, keeps me 'wake all night long. (x2)
Ain't no time for sleeping, something's always going on
   wrong.

Folks keeps yelling, "Rastus, pull the window down please. (x2)
With that snow a-falling, somebody surely going to freeze."

Hmmm, hear how that whistle blows. (x2)
It's blowing like it don't have to blow no more.

Shining shoes till morning, got no place to lay my head. (x2)
When I get through slaving, Lord, I'm almost dead.

Baby starts crying, then they takes me to be a nurse. (x2)
I gets almost drownded, and what could be worse?

Poor railroad porter, hates to leave his wife at home. (x2)
'Cause she starts to cheating just as soon as he is gone.
     (Sylvester Weaver, *Railroad Porter Blues*)

Yeah, you know it ain't but the one thing, you know, this
   black man done wrong. (x2)

Black hemp-cutter in Mercer County, Kentucky.

Yes, you know, I moved my wife and family down on Mr.
Tim Moore's farm.

Yes, you know, Mr. Tim Moore's a man,
He don't never stand and grin.
He just said, "Keep out of the graveyard,
I'll save you from the pen."
You know soon in the morning, he'll give you scrambled
    eggs.
But he's liable to call you so soon, you'll catch a mule by
    his hind legs.

Yes, you know, I got a telegram this morning,
Boy, it read, it said your wife is dead.
I showed it to Mr. Moore, he said, "Go ahead, nigger,
You know you got to plough a ridge."
That white man said, "It's raining, yeah,
It set us way behind.
I may let you bury that woman
One of these old dinner times."
I told him, "No, Mr. Moore, somebody's got to go."
He said, "If you ain't able to plough, Sam, get up there and
    grab you a hoe."
                (Lightnin' Hopkins, *Tim Moore's Farm*)

The contradictions of advanced capitalist society are felt severely
by the black working class; compared with the plight of unem-
ployment, work, even in its most alienated forms, can often
become desirable.

Hard times, hard times, hard times is going around. (x2)
Well, you know, the strike is on, baby, I believe it's going to
    carry me down.

133

No more 'joying, no more 'joying, baby, no more fun for
me. (x2)
Well, you know, my strike is on and it's trying to get the
best of me.

Well, I'm going back home, see if I can meet some of my
old friends. (x2)
Well, you know, the strike is on down here, I ain't got no
money to spend.
     (L.C. Williams, *Strike Blues*)

The contradictions were intensified during the Depression when
work was sought by millions:

Everyone's working in this town, and it's bothering me
   night and day. (x2)
It's that homewrecking crew that works for that WPA.

The landlord come this morning, knocked on my door.
He asked me wasn't I gonna pay my rent no more.
He said, "You have to move, if you can't pay."
And then he turned and walked slowly away.
So I'll have to find some other place to stay
They're gonna tear my house down, that crew from the
   WPA.

I went to the relief station, I didn't have a cent.
They said, "Stay on where you're staying, you don't have to
   pay no rent."
But when I got home, they was tacking a notice on my door.
"This house is condemned, you can't live here no more."
So a notion struck me, I'd better be on my way.
They gonna tear my house down, that crew from the WPA.

Started out next morning, I put a lock on my door.
I swore I wouldn't move, 'cause I had no place to go.
The real estate people, they all done got sore.
They won't rent to no relief clients no more.
So I know I had to walk the streets night and day.
'Cause that mean wrecking crew's coming, from the WPA.

A notion struck me, I thought I'd stay a day or two,
But I soon found out that that wouldn't do.
Early next morning while I was laying in my bed,
I heard a mighty rumbling and bricks come tumbling down
   on my head.
So I had to start ducking and dodging and be on my way.
They were tearing my house down on me, that crew from
   the WPA.
      (Casey Bill Weldon, *WPA Blues*)

But as can be seen from the preceding song and the two that follow, there were mixed feelings regarding the amount of security that even the WPA could provide.

My baby told me this morning, just about the break of
  day. (x2)
"You better get up this morning, get you a job on the WPA."

I said "I'm a gambler and I gamble night and day. (x2)
And I don't need no job on that WPA."

She said "I'm leaving you, Daddy, that's all I got to say. (x2)
I'm gonna quit my pimp, get me a man on the WPA."

So hard luck has overtaken me, have to throw my dice and
  cards away. (x2)
Have to get me a job, on that WPA.
    (Casey Bill Weldon, *New WPA Blues*)

Working on the project, what a scared man, you know. (x2)
Because everytime I look around, oooh, well, well,
  somebody's getting their 304.

Working on the project with a big furniture bill to pay. (x2)
But time I got my 304, oooh, well, well, the furniture man
  come and taken my furniture away.

Working on the project, the rent man is knocking on my
  door. (x2)
I'm sorry, Mr. Rent Man, oooh, well, well, I just got my 304.

Working on the project, my pardner got his 304, too. (x2)
So you better look out, oooh, well, well, 'cause tomorrow it
  may be you.

Working on the project, a 304 may make you cry. (x2)
There's one thing sure, oooh, well, well, you can tell the
project goodbye.
(Peetie Wheatstraw, *New Working on the Project*)

While the blues clarifies to some extent the economic position
of the black worker, we still seek a greater illumination of the
whole concept of work. The recent psychoanalytic suggestion
that work is "mentally healthy" begs the question of labor as
against alienated labor, erotic libidinal activity as against repressed
activity. The question of sublimation as against repression would

**Workers at the Mengel Box Company, Louisville, Kentucky,
1920. The Mengel Box Co. also owned the company town of
Mengelwood, Tennessee, on the outskirts of Memphis. The
town is mentioned in many blues by Memphis singers.**

seem to remain unsettled, but Marcuse (1955), following Róheim and Ferenczi, suggests that there may be a nonrepressive form of sublimation, the form of sublimation that would best describe the nature of nonalienated labor. Whether Marcuse is specifically correct or not need not concern us here. The libidinal content of work is no secret, nor is it a secret that work in its contemporary alienated forms relies extensively on repression (as well as, possibly, sublimation).

The black slang term "work" for sexual activity is not only based psychologically on the humorous reference to the *exertion* of ardent love-making, but also alludes to the erotic component of work itself, a component that sees its realization only in nonalienated forms of labor.

The connection is clear when the language of work becomes the language of love:

Drop down, baby, let me overhaul your little machine. (x2)
Well, you know, you got a loose carburetor, you been
   burning bad gasoline.

Well, I'm gonna race your motor, baby,
I'm gonna heist your hood.
Spark plugs getting old, generator ain't putting out good.
But, oooh, yeah, let me overhaul your little machine, etc.
   (Big Joe Williams, *Overhauling Blues*)

With even a vague, or unconscious, notion of the potentially enjoyable erotic character of non-alienated labor, comes the desire for a cessation of alienated labor. There is, in the blues, a strong and unmistakable desire for freedom from toil. Instead of the conservative motto "A fair day's wage for a fair day's work," the blues singers inscribe on their banner the revolutionary watchword: "Abolition of the wage system." Often, in a single verse, the singer not only establishes his identity as a worker but emphasizes his wish not to be one.

Lord, my name is written on the bosom of my shirt. (x2)
I'm a solid lover, never have to work.
> (Julius Daniels, *Richmond Blues*)

For alienated labor is recognized as one of the most destructive forces in society today: that force which contributes most to the total degeneration of humanity.

I've got the blues, I've got the blues,
I've got those misery blues.
I've got to go to work now,
Get another start,
Work is the thing that's breaking my heart,
So I've got those mean ol' misery blues.
> (Ma Rainey, *Misery Blues*)

And it is in poetic activity that alienated labor finds its most definitive negation and supersession. In the blues, the capacity for fantasy is unfaltering in its exquisite ability to unearth the desire for freedom from toil. If the last verse of the following song reintroduces the connection between erotic activity and work, ultimately the blues recognizes the tragedy of alienated labor, and its refusal is definite and final.

Ten years I worked and I can't save a dollar, and I slaved
   both day and night. (x2)
From now on, if you get me on a job, people, it'll be well,
   well after the fight.

I'm gonna stay up all night and drink and gamble, stumble
   home and take a nap. (x2)
I wouldn't tell a mule to get up, people, if he was sitting
   down in my lap.

I don't care how they laugh and tease me, I know I'll never
  break. (x2)
They just wasting their time, I wouldn't hit a lick at a snake.

I know I'll always love a woman, and I'm gonna always try
  and treat 'em right.(x2)
But 'fore one of 'em marries me off to a job it'll be a long,
  long time after the fight.
  (Mercy Dee, *After the Fight*)

THE POLICE AND THE CHURCH

> The police are the absolute enemy.
> — Charles Baudelaire

> Give us stones, brilliant stones, to drive
> off the infamous priests.
> —André Breton

Marcuse (1970:53) has suggested that "the cornerstone of psychoanalysis is the concept that social controls emerge in the struggle between instinctual and social needs . . ." We can see the emergence of such controls if we study the blues singers' reactions to two crucial instruments of repression: the police and the church. So often have these two institutions worked hand in hand toward the structuring of repressive categories within the mind as well as within society as a whole, that it becomes thematically necessary to discuss them together under one heading.

The antipathy of the police for the black working class (indeed, the working class as a whole) and vice versa is common knowledge. The police can be defined, in fact, as highly specialized defenders of existing property relations. Freud's most basic theories of super-ego formation, in simplified form (identification with parents, etc.) have passed into general acceptance. While the parents are expected to exert control over the child's behavior, the identificatory processes of super-ego formation are expected to result in an internalization of parental control. But civilization provides its own methods of control in case the process of internalization of parental authority meets with partial failure.

The connection between father, super-ego and police, well enough known not to need proof here, is evidenced by the fact that one is often replaced by the other. In some songs the police might appear in a benevolent-advisory capacity:

I heard somebody call me, it was the policeman on his beat. (x2)
Well, well, now, he just wanted to tell me, oooh, well, well,
    that I was driving on the wrong side of the street.
            (Peetie Wheatstraw, *Crazy with the Blues*)

But the role of the police, socially roughly analogous to the super-ego's role in controlling the individual's unconscious impulses, is to control *absolutely* the deepest desires and impulses of humanity. Implicit in this analogy, of course, is the connection between the working class *(contra* the police) and the id *(contra* the super-ego). The working class represents basic desires and needs, the police represent the control of these desires and needs. The control exerted by the police is senseless and merciless:

Oh, they accused me of forgery and I can't write my name.
            (Texas Alexander, *Levee Camp Moan Blues*)

Standing on the corner, talking with my brown. (x2)
Up step the policeman, take both of us down
            (Julius Daniels, *My Mamma Was a Sailor*)

It is clear to the singer that the policeman's role is not simply to restore "order" in the conventional societal sense. In a highly revealing "slip of the tongue" — of the sort on which psychoanalysis has thrown considerable light — the mayor of Chicago remarked during police atrocities against demonstrators in 1968: "The policeman is not there to create disorder; he is there to *preserve* disorder." Above all the police are hired to maintain *repression,* even in the psychoanalytic sense. In the following verse by Sleepy John Estes, the intervention of the police (the "chief") in the second line is prefaced only by an intriguing image of sexuality, and it can only be sexuality (in this verse) that elicits the association of the police (control).

I want to play marbles on my
   baby's marble ground. (x2)
I won't be worried with the
   chief, I'm gonna move out on
   the edge of town.
      (The Delta Boys, *You
       Shouldn't Do That*)

Our analogy makes clear how the police, as representatives of the super-ego and, earlier, the father, become associated with the repressive control of sexuality, and of course, aggression:

> Well, I poisoned my man, I put it in his drinking . . .
> Now, I'm in jail, and I can't keep from thinking,
> I poisoned my man, I put it in his drinking cup.
> Well, it's easy to go to jail, but, Lord, they sent me up.
>
> Bloodhounds, bloodhounds, bloodhounds is on my trail. (x2)
> They want to take me back to that cold, cold, lonesome jail.
>
> Well, I know I done wrong, but he kicked me and he
>   blacked my . . .
> I done it in a passion, I thought it was the fashion,
> I know I done wrong, but he kicked me and blacked my
>   eyes.
> But if the bloodhounds ever catch me in the electric chair
>   I'll die.
>   (Victoria Spivey, *Blood Hound Blues*)

Our discussion also makes clear how, in one sense, the working class is analogous to the unconscious or, structurally, the id. Freedom from repression, and liberation of the unconscious, is analogous to the liberation of the working class. Yet there is still more to be gained in a further application of psychoanalytic theory. Through the resolution of the oedipus complex, the young boy abandons his mother as sexual object — just as in many cases the process may not be a clear-cut example of dissolution or abandonment, the erotic as well as the hostile attachments to the father are subject to any number of instinctual fates: sublimation, repression, displacement, projection, etc. Freud (1927b:24) has shown how these defenses contribute integrally to the construction and maintenance of religion. "Thus [the child] fears [the father] no less than it longs for him and admires him. The indications of this ambivalence in the attitude toward the father are deeply imprinted in every religion . . . ." Just as the devil, historically, represented the repressed *(Minutes* 1909, no.66), in modern society, these harsher aspects of the super-ego's role are delegated to the police. The church assumes the more benevolent aspects for itself, but nonetheless remains a repressive force — in essence, in practice, in totality.

Religion has always been an agency of repression, concerning itself chiefly with the inhibition of aggression and desire, and the maintenance of guilt. It is Friedrich Nietzsche who said: "You say you believe in the necessity of religion. Be sincere! You believe in the necessity of the police!" The black church, in attempting to incorporate the more "civilizing" aspects of Christianity, has served the purposes of the ruling class by attempting to crush the spirit of revolt, replacing it with the doctrine of accommodation. Yet within the complex of psychodynamic factors that contribute to religious belief and its perpetuation, there runs the "private dialectic" of the church: hypocrisy.

> If you want to hear a preacher cuss, bake the bread, sweet
>   mama, and save him the crust. (x2)
> Preacher in the pulpit, bible in his hand, sister in corner,
>   crying, "There's my man." (x2)

Preacher come to your house, you ask him to rest his hat,
  Next thing he want to know, "Sister, where's your husband
  at?" (x2)
"Come in here, elder, shut my door, I want you to preach
  the same text you did night before." (x2)
See that preacher walking down the street, he's fixing to
  mess with every sister he meet. (x2)
Preacher, preacher, you nice and kind, I better not catch
  you at that house of mine. (x2)
      (Hi Henry Brown, *Preacher Blues*)

More than one singer — Frank Stokes, the Mississippi Sheiks,
— depicted the stereotypical deceitfulness of the black preacher,
one of the best being Joe McCoy in *Preachers Blues*.

Some folks say a preacher won't steal, but I caught three in
  my cornfield,
One had a yellow, one had a brown, looked over the mill
  and one was getting down.
Now some folks say a preacher won't steal,
But he'll do more stealing than I get regular meals.

I went to my house about half-past ten,
Looked on my bed where that preacher had been.
Now some folks say, etc.

He will eat your chicken, he will eat your pie,
He will eat your wife out on the sly.
Now some folks say, etc.

I been trying so hard, to save my life,
Just to keep that preacher from my wife.
Now some folks say, etc.

Refusing to be placated by Christianity's offer of a posthumous reward, the blues singer demands more earthly gratification.

> Take me out of this bottom before the high water rise. (x2)
> You know I ain't no Christian (preacher?), and I don't
>   wanna be baptized.
>
> I cried, Lord, my father, Lord, eh, kingdom come. (x2)
> Send me back my woman, then "thy will be done."
>   (Texas Alexander, *Justice Blues*)

In making this demand, the singer pursues the only historical reality that can offer gratification, that reality which lies outside the reality principle, but within the pleasure principle, that reality which *corresponds* to the true needs of humanity. Within such a framework, the church appears ludicrous and out of place.

> You know I went to church last night and they called on
>   po' Lightnin' to preach. (x2)
> I said, "I ain't got time, Galveston beach is over there, I'm
>   going down on the Galveston beach."
>   (Lightnin' Hopkins, *Get Off My Toe*)
>
> My mother told me, "Son, don't forget to pray."
> I fell down on my knees, I forget just what to say,
> I said, "Baaa-by."
>   (Lightnin' Hopkins, *Baby*)

Some critics, notably Oliver (1968), have suggested that the blues singers' treatment of religious themes is really quite tempered and conservative. Let us admit that there is much of radical import that is not treated in the blues; but only by carefully tracing certain themes, their development and their interconnections, does the thread of revolt which runs through the blues become properly illuminated. It is clear that this has not been

"The church . . . remains a repressive force — in essence, in practice, in totality."

Oliver's purpose, but a few words must be said about the position he espouses. A study of the poetic quality of the blues is not enhanced by the drawing up of a poetic balance sheet. Nor does the nature of revolt and more particularly of "the dialectic of negativity as the moving and generating principle" (Marx 1844:177) as it appears in the blues does not rest for its proof (as if any were needed) on the construction of a "revolutionary" balance sheet.

When Oliver suggests that in dealing with the repressive forces of the church the blues singer relies on "well worn phrases," he is undermining the dynamic nature of the whole process of negation. Having established itself in a poetic context, the appearance of "well worn phrases" in the blues must be viewed as an extremely poor gauge on which to base one's evaluations. It remains to be seen how "well worn" a phrase must become for it to be worthless; certainly the negating power of the simple "no" has lost none of its vitality throughout the centuries.

What Oliver fails to emphasize is that the very process of "negative thinking" is, in this case, fundamentally poetic. When he points out that the blues singer unoriginally concentrates his disparagement on the preacher rather than the church, thus following an older minstrel theme, he misses the point. The blues singer does not, of course, worry over the finer points of theology; I think it can safely be said that nothing is further from the thoughts of Victoria Spivey and J.B. Hutto than the contrived interpretations of Saint Augustine's *De Civitae Dei* which so troubled the medieval scholastics. The blues critique, emphatically materialist, is directed not against heavenly abstractions (God, Jesus, the Holy Ghost) but against the hypocrisy and pretension of the pompous self-appointed "representatives" of God on earth. Nothing would be more false, however, than to suggest that the blues is therefore not opposed to religion as such, but only to this or that organized religious institution, or (still worse) to suggest that the blues itself is some sort of "secular religion" [*sic*]. The entire spirit of the blues is antithetical to this cheap and sentimental agnostic reformism. The blues does not intervene on the theological plane with the obsolete tools of rationalism or in the name of some empty "humanism." On the contrary, it enters the fray wholeheartedly *on the side of Evil.* The "devil's music" is the denunciation of everything religion stands for and the glorification of everything religion condemns. The blues singer could say, as the black surrealist poet Aimé Cesaire (1939:76) said in his *Return to My Native Land,* speaking for all those of African descent throughout the world, "I have assassinated God with my laziness with my words with my gestures with my obscene songs." The blues is uncompromisingly atheistic. It has no interest in the systems of divine reward and punishment: it holds out for "paradise now."

This "evil" aspect of the blues is wholly in keeping with the course of all authentic poetry. As William Blake said in his *Marriage of Heaven and Hell,* "The reason Milton wrote in fetters when he wrote of Angels and God, and at liberty when of devils and Hell, is because he was a true Poet and of the devil's party without knowing it." More than one blues singer could be said to have made a pact with the devil. The great Peetie Wheatstraw, drawing on a long tradition of Negro folklore, proclaimed himself the Devil's Son-in-Law and the High Sheriff from Hell. In Robert Johnson's *Me and the Devil* we find the line: "Hello, Satan, I believe it's time to go." And Julia Moody in her *Mad Mama's Blues* (quoted elsewhere in these pages) said of herself: "I'm the devil in disguise, got murder in my eyes."

CRIME

> Criminals have blue hands.
> — René Crevel

The blues singers' critique of repressive institutions often goes even further and frequently enjoys highly imaginative detours. A number of blues lyrics, for example, must be considered deliberate repudiations of "law and order" and even outright celebrations of crime.

I didn't build this world, but I sure can tear it down.
(Pleasant Joe, *Sawmill Man Blues*)

Yes, you know my mama told me
The day that I left her door.
She said, "You gonna have bad luck, Son,
And I don't care where you go."
I said "Just bring me my shotgun,
Boys, you can bring just one or two shells.
Yes, if I don't get some competition,
You know, it's got to be trouble here."
(Lightnin' Hopkins, *Shotgun Blues*)

The Second Chicago Fire Under the Direction of Elmore James (1975) by Jean-Jacques Jack Dauben.

Many blues singers (among them Lightnin' Hopkins, Bukka White, Hogman Maxey and Robert Pete Williams) have served time in prison. Every detail of the horror of prison life — a horror multiplied a thousandfold for poor blacks in the South — is powerfully chronicled in the blues.

Judge give me life this morning down on Parchman Farm. (x2)
I wouldn't hate it so bad, but I left my wife' n' moan.

I'm down on old Parchman Farm and sure want to go back
  home. (x2)
But I hope some day, I will overcome.
      (Bukka White, *Parchman Farm Blues*)

Now it's Eighteen Hundred and Ninety Three,
I got arrested off of Beale Street.
I went 'fore the judge, I said, "Judge, what is my fine?"
"A hundred dollars fine and eleven twenty-nine."
"Now, look here, judge, can't you hold up off of that fine?"
He said, "Go ahead on, nigger, that ain't no great long
  time."
      (Memphis Jug Band, *Snitchin' Gambler Blues*)

You see my mama,
Tell her for me·
I got life-time in prison,
I'll never go free.

I hate to hear that big bell ring. (x2)
So many years in prison, hobbled down with ball and chain.

You oughta been in prison, Big Brazos, the year 19 and 4. (x2)
See a dead man laying on every turnrow.
      (Smokey Hogg, *Penitentiary Blues*)

But poetry is itself a crime within the framework of bourgeois Christian values, and for this reason the blues songs that glorify crime retain a special quality of enticement. For in certain conditions the working-class criminal embodies sentiments and inclinations which are primitively but fundamentally revolutionary. Baby Boy Warren sang:

> Bring me my machine-gun, bring me two or three belts of
> balls. (x2)
> I wants to go and free my baby from behind the
> penitentiary walls.
> *(Baby Boy Blues)*

It is relatively rare, of course (and could not have been otherwise) for this radical individualism in the blues to evolve into a *class* consciousness. But J. B. Lenoir, in his *Everybody Wants to Know* (a variation of his controversial *Eisenhower Blues*) threatened the ruling class with theft and by implication, with expropriation:

> You rich people listen, you better listen real deep,
> If we poor peoples get so hungry we gonna get some food
> to eat.

But perhaps the most lyrically exalted defense of the criminal's anti-authoritarian conception of life was sung by Bessie Smith:

> Back in Black Mountain a child will smack your face. (x2)
> Babies crying for liquor, and all the birds sing bass.
>
> Black Mountain people are bad as they can be. (x2)
> They uses gunpowder just to sweeten their tea.
>
> On the Black Mountain, can't keep a man in jail. (x2)
> If the jury find him guilty, the judge will go his bail.

Had a man in Black Mountain, sweetest man in town. (x2)
He met a city gal, and he throwed me down.

I'm bound for Black Mountain, me and my razor and my
   gun. (x2)
I'm going to shoot him if he stands still and cut him if he
   runs.

Down in Black Mountain, they all shoot quick and straight. (x2)
A bullet will get you if you start to dodging too late.

Got the devil in my soul, and I'm full of bad booze. (x2)
I'm out here for trouble, I've got the Black Mountain Blues.
         (Black Mountain Blues)

MAGIC

> Magic ceremonies, psychic exercises
> leading to concentration and ecstasy, the
> liberation of mental automatism, the
> simulation of morbid attitudes, are so
> many means capable, through the tension
> they induce, of refining the vision, of
> enlarging the normal faculties; they are ways
> of approach to the realm of the marvelous.
> — Pierre Mabille

The chains of repression are dealt with by the blues singer in
other ways as well. According to Róheim (1930:v), "it is by *magic*
that man takes the offensive against the world at large." And in
the blues we encounter an insistence on the power of magic in
the form of various spells, charms, and rituals.

She had a red flannel rag, talking about hoo-dooin' poor
  me. (x2)
Well, I believe I'll go to Froggy Bottom so she will let me be.
    (Alex Moore, *Goin' Back to Froggy Bottom*)

Despite a probable common origin, magic and religion are fundamentally dissimilar — the differences are especially evident when the religion in question is Catholicism or another form of Christianity. The surrealist Benjamin Péret (1943:63), in discussing the evolution of myth as well as the evolution of religion from magic, has said "Innumerable generations have added the diamonds they discovered as well as the dull metal they mistook for gold." For Péret, Christ is the dull metal. He continues: "While it is true that poetry grows in the rich earth of magic, the pestilential miasmas of religion rise from the same ground and poison poetry. . . ." Péret then relates the myths of "great poetic exuberance" of certain tribes to their lack of moral precepts. "On the other hand, more evolved people see their myths lose their poetic brilliance while multiplying their moral restrictions." Alienation and religious morality are the enemies of poetry and desire! Through magic, the rational and the irrational, the subjective and objective become whole again, poetically prefiguring the dialectical resolution of all the dualisms rooted in class society. Poetry is created by the destruction of the barrier that separates the wish from its fulfillment, the dream from waking life. The blues songs of magic and superstition compel our attention through their links with poetic activity. "In the language of magic, different grammatical forms are used because . . . the magic of language was evolved on the basis of the magic of love" (Róheim 1943:100).

My pistol may snap,
My mojo is frail,
Ah, but I rub my root,
My luck will never fail.

When I rub my root, my John the Conqueror root.
Aww, you know, there ain't nothing she can do, Lord,
I rub my John the Conqueror root.

I was accused of murder,
In the first degree.
The judge's wife cried,
"Let the man go free."
I was rubbing my root, etc.

Oh, I can get in a game,
Don't have a dime.
All I have to do is rub my root,
I win every time.
When I rub my root, etc.
(Muddy Waters, *My John the Conqueror Root*)

The revelation of the often unconscious meaning of such "lucky objects" (John the Conqueror root = penis) is but the revelation of desire. Often magic is called on when frustration threatens desire.

I'm going to Louisiana, get me a mojo hand. (x2)
I'm gonna fix my woman so she can't have no other man.
(Lightnin' Hopkins, *Mojo Hand*)

They say it's bad luck when you see a black cat cross the
street. (x2)
Ah, the black cat must have slept in my bed, oooh, Lord,
the black snake must have crawled across my feet.
(Big Bill Broonzy, *Bad Luck Man*)

Many blues singers were (and in some cases still are) attracted to certain aspects of *voodoo* and its attendant rituals. This is not the place to attempt a detailed discussion of the complex subject of voodoo.[11] But it is worth noting that it is still widely practiced today: not only in Haiti and throughout the Caribbean but also in the U.S., and not only in New Orleans but in the black ghettoes of the North. Of course it has undergone extensive modification over the years, but even today in Chicago one can still find shops displaying for sale numerous magic powders, potions, talismans — "Attraction Powder," "Uncrossing Powder," "Black Cat Oil," "Hex-Removing Floor-Wash," John the Conqueror Root, etc. — as well as an impressive array of popular dream-books (the *Napoleon Mascot,* the *Three Witches,* etc.) more or less voodoo in origin.

Several scholarly studies of voodoo can be recommended (Rigaud 1970; Deren 1952; Tallant 1946; and Metraux 1972) while Oliver (1960) has briefly surveyed voodoo traces in the blues. The most stimulating suggestions toward a fundamentally new interpretation of voodoo, however, have come not from traditional anthropologists or scholars but rather from poets and painters, above all the surrealists. André Breton was able to witness voodoo rites in Haiti (a rare privilege for whites); his deep appreciation of their significance was clearly derived from his poetic affinity with the mental processes involved.[12] Surrealism, in permitting us to see voodoo in a new light, also enhances our appreciation of yet another aspect of the blues — for, to a far greater extent than anyone has conceded, the blues may be viewed as a vehicle for the expression of voodoo. More specifically, the voodoo trance state, in which the subject is seized by powers "from below," approaches the "pure psychic automatism" of surrealism; and the blues, too, in its improvisatory intensity in the heat of inspiration, also draws on these same powers "from below." In this regard it is interesting to see Michel Leiris (1946:148) remark, in a discussion of jazz in the surrealist milieu in the 1920s — and the same could certainly be said of the blues — that "it functioned magically, and its means of influence can be compared to a kind of possession." Once again we are able to observe the intimate connection — here the link is entrancement — between ancient primitive magical traditions, the blues, and the most audacious and revolutionary current of modern poetry and thought.

The evidence of voodoo in the blues is not limited to a certain identity of spiritual values. On the contrary, the lyrics of blues songs reveal a profound and enduring preoccupation with voodoo themes and imagery. Blues singers refer constantly to voodoo, "hoo-doo," mojos and all sorts of magical apparatus. It would be futile here to attempt to distinguish between specifically voodoo elements and magical elements derived from other sources; Curtis Jones clears up this confusion:

I call it black magic, some call it plain hoodoo.
(Black Magic Blues)

Black cats, black snakes, black cat bones, all appear frequently in the blues. Yet often our interest is heightened by references which seem more obscure. In the darkest corners of the mind, the shadowy vestiges of totemism flourish. Frogs, for example, are occasionally mentioned in the blues, usually in a most enigmatic fashion.

If I had wings like the bullfrog on the pond.
(Yank Rachel, T-Bone Steak Blues)

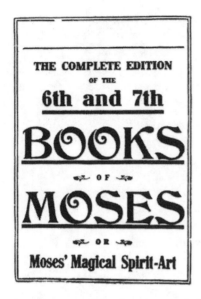

THE COMPLETE EDITION
OF THE
6th and 7th
BOOKS
OF
MOSES
OR
Moses' Magical Spirit-Art

NEW KEY TO FIND YOUR OWN NUMBERS
BASED ON SYSTEMS OF THE ANCIENTS

AUNT SALLY'S
POLICY PLAYERS
DREAM BOOK

STUDY OF HARMONY IN NUMBERS

But the use of the frog in magic is less obscure, and may throw some light on references to frogs in the blues.

Many "lucky charms" and mixtures involve frogs and toads, or parts of them, and this association is by no means confined to America. Daraul (1962:133) describes ceremonies involving the Labord witches in which a large number of these witches went to the cemetery to baptize toads which were dressed for the purpose in red or black velvet with bells at their neck or feet. Summers (1926:157) reports similar ceremonies. Numerous beliefs and rituals in Europe, Africa, and America show that the frog and toad are associated with the production of rain (Frazer 1911: 292; Pucket 1926: 321, 507); others use frogs and toads for their curative powers (Frazer 1913:50; Puckett 1926:364-5, 374). Symbolically, we have been told that the frog represents the womb, vagina or mother (Róheim 1930:90) or the penis (Silberer 1917: 225), although the latter author suggest that a *toad* may be the uterus. Róheim's findings are the result of analyses of numerous rain-making rituals which include frogs, while

Silberer's thesis, at least regarding the frog, draws support from a rather common fairy-tale theme, with which we are all familiar. To quote Jones (1931:70), "There is . . . a large class of fairy tales in which the wonderful prince appears first in disguise as a frog . . . or any other animal, to disclose his true nature at the appropriate moment. Ricklin has clearly shown how the gradual overcoming of the resistance to sexuality is represented by the releasing from the spell in these stories, i.e., the release from guilt and disgust."

Associated with this material are two beliefs which Puckett (1926:551, 481) suggests are common to a number of blacks in the American South. The devil may appear as a toad, and a toad in the house means death. Notwithstanding the distinctions between frogs and toads which may or may not find their way into the various rituals involving them, these two beliefs may throw some light on some of the blues lines which refer to frogs, and which until now have appeared quite puzzling. If unconsciously the frog may represent the penis, or womb, vagina or mother, and if a frog may consciously represent the devil or death, the following extracts lose none of their remarkability but only some of their enigmatic status.

Have you ever woke up with them bullfrogs on your mind?
    (William Harris, *Bullfrog Blues*)

Hey, hey, hey, hey,
Bullfrog blues is really on my mind.
They're all in my bedroom drinking up my wine.

Hey, pretty papa, hey pretty papa,
I can't stand these bulifrog blues no more.
They're all in my cabinets, hopping all over my clothes.

I woke up this morning to make a fire in my stove. (x2)
Bullfrogs in my breakfast, (making their?) jelly roll.

Hey, Mr. Bullfrog, I'm gonna tell you all,
I can't stand your jelly-rolling here.
You can go out in the back-yard, I'll make a pallet there.

I will make you a pallet so you can jelly roll. (x2)
And you can cook my breakfast right on my brand new
    stove.
                    (Jenny Pope, *Bull Frog Blues*)

In this last song, there even seems to be a parallel to the fairy
story mentioned by Jones — what is first rejected as undesirable
("I can't stand . . .") is in the last verse welcomed ("You can cook
my breakfast right on my brand new stove"). In the last three
verses, the sexual significance of the frog is unmistakable.

In other songs, the frog is obviously an image for the male or
the penis, as in J. T. Smith's *Hopping Toad Blues:*

I'll hop down in your basement, don't mean to harm a
    single soul. (x2)
I'll shake all of your ashes and shovel you in some brand
    new coal.

I don't have no friends, by myself I'm always on the road. (x2)
Just let me hop you one time, mama, and you'll keep me
    for your little toad.

Mama, would you let a poor little old toad frog dive down
    in your water pond. (x2)
I'll dive down and come right out and I won't stay in your
    water long.

Mama, don't you know one thing, your water tank is just
    deep enough. (x2)
I can dive down to the bottom, take my time and tread
    right back up.

Other beliefs often find their sources revealed through other songs. Compare Howlin' Wolf's *I Ain't Superstitious* with Lightnin' Hopkins' *Lonesome Dog*. In Lightnin' Hopkins' song, the dog howls after the death of his owner.

> I got a dog in my back yard howls every day my baby's
>   gone. (x2)
> You know, he puts my mind on a wonder, I begin to think
>   what's going on wrong.

> Yeah, you know things is getting sad when a dog feel it
>   deep down in his heart. (x2)
> Yes, you know a man can't help but miss his rider when the
>   dog in his back yard hate to see them part.

In Howlin' Wolf's song, the howling dog is a *portent* of death.

> Well, the dogs all howl all over the neighborhood. (x2)
> That is a true sign of death, baby, that ain't no good.

The image of the dog howling after his owner's death or departure becomes the image of death as signalled by a howling dog. Indeed, the blues not only provides us with an endless variety of images, but also reveals numerous keys to their symbolic content. The next chapter will be devoted to a discussion of these symbols and images as well as their meanings; for now, we have only to add that the power of poetry rests not on its analyzability, but on its power to convulse, to invoke desire, to supersede conventional conceptions of reality, to liberate the capacity for fantasy, to set free the images of magic and desire.

> I don't want my rooster crowing after the sun goes down. (x2)
> Don't bring peanuts in my house, it will make a coffin turn
>   around.

I don't want nobody to put their bare hands on my head. (x2)
I don't eat everybody's cooking, I am suspicious of my
    cornbread.

Don't touch me with your broom, don't let my lamp get
    low. (x2)
Don't let the dogs start to howling 'cause somebody got to
    go.

Take your hat off of my bed and hang it on a nail. (x2)
If I sit down on your trunk, I am bound to go to jail.

I don't want my brother to put his bare feets in my shoes. (x2)
Somebody stole my rabbit's foot, and I've got the suspicious
    blues.
                (Jazz Gillum, *The Blues What Am*)

Superstitions may be restrictive of human freedom just as are the
dogmas of Christianity. Yet the differences as elucidated by Péret
remain inescapable. Superstitions reveal less alienated mental
processes and a closer contact with the unconscious. This quality of magic thinking is clarified by an example provided by
Freud (1901:259-60). "The Roman who gave up an important
undertaking if he saw an ill-omened flight of birds was . . . in a
relative sense justified; his behavior was consistent with his
premises. But if he withdrew from the undertaking because he
had stumbled on the threshold of his door . . . he was also in an
absolute sense superior to us unbelievers; he was a better psy-
chologist than we are striving to be. For his stumbling must have
revealed to him the existence of a doubt, a counter-current at
work within him, whose force might at the moment of execu-
tion subtract from the force of his intentions. For we are only
sure of complete success if all our mental forces are united in
striving towards the desired goal." Of course, the close relationship between magical thinking and the more primary processes

succeeds in unearthing the source of powerful and fantastic imagery, which by its nature reintroduces the concept of poetry.

In magic, there is poetry — religion poisons poetry. The surrealists have long argued that one exceedingly crucial task of modern poetic activity is the dechristianization of the world. There is no poetry of religion. There is only poetry of revolt — revolt against the degradation of language, against the repressive forces of the church, the police, the family and the ruling class, against the inhibition of sexuality and aggression, against the general repugnance of everyday life. As we have said, the songs do not always depict liberation, but even when they do not, they invoke an insistence on the instinctual and unconscious, an insistence which is at once revelatory of the poetic process and destructive of the techniques of academic depreciation and dissection. The blues songs reveal indelible traces of humanity's original grandeur, and by comparison, they indict the ludicrous spectacle of modern civilization.

MENTAL MECHANISMS

> Only the analogical switch arouses our passion,
> only by it can we start the world's motor.
> — André Breton

The preceding discussion has been devoted to the content of blues songs. In closing the consideration of this subject, I would like to make a few remarks about several psychological mechanisms which contribute to verse structure. These include forgetting (repressing), suppressing, repetition, elaboration, and wish-fulfillment (which contributes to all of these).

The subject of wish-fulfillment has been broached each time we have mentioned desire. It is the unconscious wish that can cause a singer to forget a line or verse, or, more or less "automatically," substitute another in its place. It is the conscious wish that can cause the singer intentionally to substitute one verse for another, although unconscious wishes may hold the only answer as to why the discarded verse was felt to be unsuitable.

Freud has made clear that forgetting occurs when the material in question becomes linked to unpleasurable unconscious material. This explains in part the alterations that a number of songs undergo in the process of their evolution. Additionally, song-texts are often changed to "suit the singer," i.e., the singer alters the lyrics consciously in an effort to make the song better fit his social circumstances or his psychic state.

The mechanism of repetition helps us to understand the structure of the blues. Our earlier discussion of mastery suggests that there is more to be said regarding the notion that the "standard" structure of a blues verse — the first two lines identical, the third different but rhyming — evolved solely out of the practical consideration that having a second line identical to the first gives the singer more time to think up a third line! Considering the part played by repetition in our psychic life and above all its manifestations in creative activity, it is likely that one determinant of the evolution of this verse structure, coming as it does (according to some authorities) from an earlier form wherein all three lines were identical, is the *psychological tendency toward repetition,* whether it relates to mastery of unpleasant undischarged affects, repetition of what is pleasurable in itself, or a more all-encompassing "repetition compulsion" in the sense in which Freud posited it. What is important is that we understand that the repetition is determined psychically (internally) as well as mechanically (externally). (For a fascinating discussion of related material, see Goja (1920), "The Alteration of Folk Songs by Frequent Singing: A Contribution to the Psychology of Folk Poetry.")

The repetition of the first line may become for many singers what Szekely (1967:353) calls the "creative pause." "By the expression 'creative pause' is meant the time interval beginning from the moment the thinker interrupts conscious preoccupation with his unsolved problem and ending when the solution of the problem or the insight suddenly and unexpectedly presents itself." He goes on to suggest that "the length of a creative pause can vary widely. In the production of a witticism, for example, it can last a few seconds or even only for the fraction of a second, so that the occurrence of a creative pause is not observed." So it may be in the blues, where the repetition of the first line offers for some a supreme distraction, a sense of non-preoccupation, where the mind ranges freely beyond the confines of reality and where verses become resolved with a peculiar ease. Such is the nature of "automatic" thinking.

Notes

[1] An example of this sort of academic obscurantism may be found in Neil Leonard's *Jazz and the White Americans* (1962:170-2). Or again, in his study of Charlie Patton, John Fahey subjects us to a enumeration of "happy," "sad" and "neutral" images in Patton's songs.

[2] None of this is to deny the utter horror and degradation of black life in America, or that the realities of life for the working-class black lie at the core of the blues. But the ample coverage of this exceedingly significant area in Paul Oliver's *Blues Fell This Morning* makes further discussion of it unnecessary here. The area in which Oliver's book is deficient, the exploration of factors other than the socio-economic ones, forms the essential network of exploration for this volume.

[3] "Blues as poetry . . . was another well-intentioned romance on our part. There are blues singers who might be considered poets" *if* their images are chosen "with sufficient care to bear repetition on the printed page" Guralnick (1971:22-23).

[4] Some critics immediately recognized this quality. Bucklin Moon wrote, "There is no doubt that there is in [the blues] a strong condemnation of the ruling caste which could never be spoken to a white man's face . . . Underneath is a militant protest . . ."(1953:9).

[5] As a related example, we can suggest that the many blues dealing with the subject of war but made during peacetime, which have been considered enigmatic simply because of their temporal incongruity are actually reflections of a psychic reality, and it is from this fact alone that they achieve their meaningfulness. It cannot be said that

war songs became popular during the war and just stayed in a performer's repertoire. There is a reason such a song was maintained and the reason is psychological: many wishes and fears, with all their attendant symbolizations and representations, unconscious and conscious, regarding war, peace and the president, do not necessarily lose their psychical value simply because the war ends. Indeed, such values may change through the course of historical and personal incident, but the subjects themselves (war, etc.) maintain a psychic value which need not vaguely harmonize with reality, but which can always be expected to exert a powerful influence on song-making.

6 Painful emotions are aroused and the attempt to suppress them proves superfluous. In simple terms, this is the mechanism that produces laughter in the joke, but it is rare that we find actual jokes in the blues. An exception to this, and there are others, is Barbecue Bob's riddle in *Good Time Rounder:*

There's 25 women in this hotel with me, you and your brother, what time would it be? (x2)

That's very easy, mama, be 25 after 3.

7 Paul Garon, "The Dirty Dozen" in *Living Blues* 97 (May/June, 1991).

8 How then, might one ask, does Rod Gruver (1970), in "Blues as Secular Religion," arrive at the conclusion that in the blues women are treated by the male blues singers as "goddesses"?

9 It is interesting to note that the blues' affinity for the night is retained also in the most revolutionary currents in jazz — evidenced in the bebop of the '40s, when two of the leading works were *Night in Tunisia* and *Round Midnight,* as well as in the more recent innovations associated with John Coltrane, Ornette Coleman, Cecil Taylor and others. This affinity, however, is noticeably absent from other musical forms today.

10 This is not the place to attempt a more thorough discussion of work and play. For a further elucidation of the question, I recommend the works of Marx, Fourier, Winnicott (1971) and Marcuse (1955).

11 For a voodoo reading of the blues, see Julio Finn, *The Bluesman* (London: Quartet Books, 1986), (Brooklyn: Interlink, 1992).

12 For an introduction to the surrealists' perspective on voodoo see particularly Breton's essay on the Haitian voodoo painter Hector Hyppolite (1947); Pierre Mabille's *Le Miroir du merveilleux* (1962); the poetry of Haitian Clement Magloire-Saint-Aude and the

Martiniquan Aimé Cesaire (1939), as well as the works of the Cuban surrealist painter Wifredo Lam. See also Michel Leiris' essay "On the Use of Catholic Religious Prints by Practitioners of Voodoo in Haiti" (1960). For a brilliant discussion of voodoo from the angle of poetic creation see the essay "The Writer and Society" by the Guyanese Wilson Harris (1967).

symbols, images & the dream

Have you ever dreamed lucky, woke up
cold in hand?
— William Harris, *Bullfrog Blues*

SYMBOL AND IMAGE

> It is in the essence of symbols to be symbolic.
> — Jacques Vaché

> The image is a pure creation of the mind.
> — Pierre Reverdy

Previous studies (Oliver 1960, 1968; Charters 1963; Oster 1969) have dwelt at some length on the use of symbols and imagery in the blues. While to many the difference between an image and a symbol may seem to be an academic one, and in most studies such distinctions have been drawn along the feeblest of academic lines — often with no other purpose in mind than the assignation of terms to various devices (Charters 1963) — in our investigation we find that the necessity to distinguish between the two takes on the nature of an imperative, essential to our clarification of the relationship between repression and the blues.

It would be worthwhile at this point to clarify a few factors concerning repression in its psychological sense. Repression refers to unconscious material which is, for all practical purposes, incapable of becoming conscious. What is repressed is unconscious, not just temporarily unthought of, or temporarily forgotten. The concept of repression is crucial for the understanding of symbolization, for only what is repressed is, or needs to be, symbolized (Jones 1916:116). Our definition of a symbol, then, will be a narrower one than is encountered in everyday conversation; it will be a psychoanalytic one, for it is only by applying such a seemingly restrictive, *precise* definition that we can come to understand the various levels of mental functioning and their role in the blues. Symbols are distinct from metaphors, similes, or other such figures.

> Only such things (or ideas) are symbols in the sense of psychoanalysis as are invested in consciousness with a logically inexplicable and unfounded affect, and of which it may be analytically established that they owe this affective over-emphasis to *unconscious* identification with another thing (or idea), to which the surplus of affect really belongs. Not all similes, therefore, are symbols, but only those in which the one member of the equation is repressed into the unconscious. (Ferenzci 1913b: 277-8)

Ferenczi goes on to quote Rank and Sachs who suggest that a symbol is "a special kind of indirect representation which is distinguished by certain peculiarities from other allied kinds, such as the simile, the metaphor, the allegory, the allusion, and other forms of figurative representation of thought material . . ." and "it is a substitutive, illustrative replacement-expression for something *hidden* [emphasis added]." Following Jones we must add that symbols have universal meaning.

Freud and his co-workers in 1920. Back row, left to right: Otto Rank, Karl Abraham, Max Eitingon, Ernest Jones; front row: Freud, Sandor Ferenczi, Hanns Sachs.

What is most significant is that symbolization involves something hidden, something repressed, yet universal in its meaning. The affect originally attached to an object or idea (for example, the father) becomes displaced onto another object (for example, the president) but the original affective attachment (and connection) is repressed. The whole process of symbolization is unconscious, and the user of symbols does not necessarily know that he is employing them.

Images, like symbols, need not involve repression, and the implications of this distinction are considerable. We could say that images constitute a variable element superimposed on symbols themselves; as the surrealist Virgil Teodorescu (1970:34) wrote: "It is the *constant* aspect of the symbol which makes possible affective links between human beings. This constant element is a permanent psychological function, and the variable element represents the ever-renewed relationship of the indi-

171

vidual with the environment." The differences are made clear by an example of how an idea or object can at once be a symbol as well as an image or sign. Jones (1916) cites the wedding ring, for it is a *symbol* of the female genital, i.e., it signifies the female genital in the unconscious. Although common parlance implies that the ring is a *symbol* of fidelity, etc., it is clearly not a *symbol* for this latter concept, but perhaps merely, as Jones suggests, an emblem. In this example, the symbolic (unconscious, hidden, repressed) meaning of the ring is the female genital; the ring also represents, *to the conscious mind,* ideas related to fidelity, love, devotion, etc., and for these ideas we may say that the ring is an emblem or a sign. The *image* of a wedding ring may invoke its symbolic content or its emblematic content, yet we may say that when the symbolic content is not relevant (or existent), we are dealing with an image.[1]

Bearing in mind the distinction between the symbol and other forms of indirect representation, we are reminded that according to Freud (1900:351) symbolization is even more evident in folklore than in dreams. Some years later *(Minutes* 1909, no.73), Freud also suggested that in spite of our resistances to the interpretation of certain symbols as they manifest themselves in dreams and waking life, we are quite prepared to recognize the hidden meaning of the same symbols when they occur in jokes, sayings, couplets, and, we might add, the blues. For in the blues (as well as in certain jokes and proverbs), the hidden meaning of the symbol is liberated and set free — the symbol becomes an image, and repression disappears. The original affective attachment is no longer repressed.

This house is full of stinging snakes, crawling all in my bed.(x2)
I can't rest at night from them crawling all under my head.

I got up this morning, one stung me on my leg. (x2)
I can't sleep at night because they keeps me awake.

Ummmm, wonder where my stinging snake gone? (x2)
I can't see no peace since my stinging snake left my home.
  (Memphis Minnie, *Stinging Snake Blues*)

Hmmm, black snake crawling in my room (x2)
Some pretty mama better come and get this black snake soon.

Hmmm, what's the matter now? (x2)
Sugar, what's the matter? "Don't like no black snake nohow."

Hmmm, wonder where's my black snake gone? (x2)
Black snake, mama, done run my darling home.
  (Blind Lemon Jefferson, *The Black Snake Moan*)

The symbolic (unconscious) meaning of the snake (penis) which is revealed through the analysis of dreams, phobias, folklore and myths, appears time and time again in the blues — unrepressed and conscious, an image of the singer's desire, its symbolic meaning no longer secret.

Numerous symbols for the penis, perhaps unrecognized by us in our own mental activities, see their conscious realization in the blues.

Oh, my bull's in the pasture, babe, Lord, where there's no grass. (x2)
I swear every minute seems like it's gonna be my last.

And my bull's got a horn long as my arm. (x3)

I throw a five-pound axe and I cut three different ways. (x2)
And I cut for the women both night and day.

I throw a five-pound axe and I just dropped in your town. (x2)
I got weight enough behind me to (drive that ol') axe on down.
     (Charlie Patton, *Jersey Bull Blues*)

I got a ten-pound hammer and I just dropped in your town. (x2)
I got weight behind it for to drive this ol' hammer on down.

I got a ten-pound hammer and I got weight to drive it down. (x2)
I drive for the women from town to town.

I got a ten-pound hammer,
  the women love to hear it
  sound. (x2)
They says, "Come on, Moses,
  go and drive it down."
(Mose Andrews, *Ten Pound
  Hammer*)

Interestingly enough, the phallic symbolism of the snake often fades behind the force of a consciously wrought image determined, it is true, by its own unconscious sources. In this line by Memphis Minnie, "There's a boa constrictor and a lemon stick" *('Frisco Town)*, the "lemon stick" is an image of the penis, and the snake, by virtue of its being a *constrictor,* an image of the vagina. The singer's conscious use of this image should suggest that, in the unconscious as well, certain snakes may indeed be regarded as representing the vagina and not the penis.[2]

The blues contains many symbolic references; it suffices to cite only one or two others. It was already suggested that in the Charlie McCoy verse cited in the discussion of travel the train is a *symbol* for the father. If we recall a common verse like Willie Love's, in which the train is used as a conscious image for a competitive male —

74 is just a freight train, but it's got ways just like a man. (x2)
Well it'll take your sweet little woman, boys, and let you
  down cold in hand.
  (Seventy Four Blues)

SYMBOL OF THE CROWNED SERPENT

WITH ITS

MAGICAL HIEROGLYPHICS.

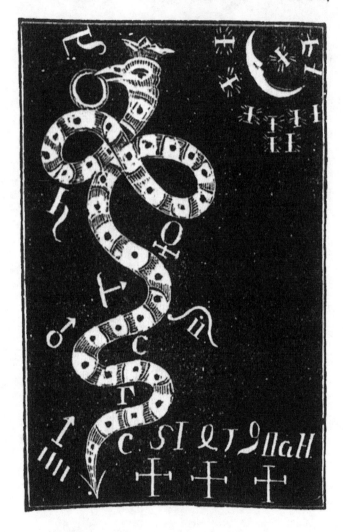

and if we recall that the father is the male child's original source of competition, our evaluation of the symbolic (hidden, unconscious) meaning of McCoy's verse (train = superior strength = father) becomes more intelligible.

The symbolic value of fishing (to the unconscious, fishing means birth, intercourse, or both) finds its open and conscious expression in the Memphis Jug Band's *Fishing in the Dark:*

Now look here, when I go fishing, it ain't no crime,
When I'm fishing, I'm fishing after something of mine.
Aw, fishing in the dark,
Aw, fishing in the dark,
Aw, fishing in the dark,
Honey, that's my birthmark.

Goin' down to the river, jump in the spring,
I catch the first (perch?) fish, it don't mean a thing.
Aw, fishing in the dark, etc.

Tell my Ma, tell my Pa,
Would stop fishing, but I can't say "Naw."
Fishing in the dark, etc.

Tell all you people what it's all about,
Can't catch a catfish, I'll catch a trout.
Aw, fishing in the dark, etc.

This song provides an excellent example of the various levels of mental functioning operative in the blues. While we have shown that numerous symbols function in the blues as conscious images, it must be borne in mind that the blues also contains true symbols, as well as other references of unconscious significance. While the listener can consciously enjoy the singer's references to sexual activity (fishing), it is doubtful if either singers or listeners are consciously aware of the relationship between fishing

Fishing on the Mississippi, 1947.

and birth, in spite of the recurrence of "that's my birthmark" in
the refrain. The refrain does confirm the existence of the symbolic equation fishing = birth, but while "fishing in the dark"
becomes an *image* for intercourse, it remains a *symbol* for birth.

The conscious level on which some songs operate may be
ambiguous, as in Memphis Minnie's *North Memphis Blues:*

> I'll tell all you people, you can rest (at ease? and eat?)
> You don't have to worry about cooking, go to North
>   Memphis Café and eat.
> I'll tell all you people, you can rest at ease.
> Because the North Memphis Café got everything you really
>   need.
>
> I don't buy no wood, even buy no coal,
> I go to North Memphis Café and eat and don't be a dope,

I tell all you people, etc.
You don't have to worry about cooking, go to North
   Memphis Café and eat.

I'm gonna tell you all something, I don't change like the
   wind.
If you go to the North Memphis Café and eat, you'll go
   back again.
I'll tell, etc.

Now listen to me, good people, I don't aim to make you
   mad
You go to the North Memphis Café and get something you
   never had.
I'll tell, etc.

There might be initial disagreement on whether or not
Memphis Minnie intended the song to be sexually suggestive.
An argument in favor of the thesis that she did is the last line,
"get something you never had," a line which she used many
times in other songs, always in an openly sexual way. But assuming that we do not know her conscious intentions, and assuming that her listeners gain conscious pleasure from the song,
simply as a song about a café, it is undeniable that the café may
have to the unconscious of the singer, as well as to the unconscious of the listener, another meaning, i.e., our original source
of nourishment — the mother, or more specifically the breast;
by displacement the café might also come to represent the
female genital. The unconscious meaning is the *latent content* of
the song.
   In spite of the many resistances that this sort of interpretation
inevitably calls forth, it is further an established fact that both listener and singer gain satisfaction from the latent content of a
song, even when such content remains latent (unconscious) and
never becomes manifest (conscious). The importance of this fact

Monroe, Louisiana, 1947.

should not be underestimated; the latent content of all creative activity contributes in large measure to its capacity to be enjoyed. Indeed, art has often been defined in terms of its ability to express the "universal forbidden wishes of mankind," and the blues is no exception. The uniqueness of the blues is due to its manner of expressing these same wishes, a manner in which wishes often kept hidden are openly proclaimed.

In spite of the fact that the blues deals with commonly unconscious material in a uniquely unrepressed way, there is also in the blues unconscious material. This is a simple fact, and it implies only that the blues singer suffers, as do we all, from repression; it in no way discredits our thesis that the blues operates on a poetic level that is to an unusual extent free from repression.

Unfortunately, the unique nature of the blues has generated certain difficulties of interpretation, all of which are strongly reinforced by the tendency toward anti-intellectualism which is predominant in the "youth culture" from which the blues has drawn many of its newest followers. No doubt reinforced in their own anti-intellectualism by years of exposure to vacuous academic attempts to "analyze" poems, many of them seem to resist any attempt to understand the blues. For them, the blues is not poetry, not protest or revolt — it is not anything, really; just "the blues" — that's all. And in their resistances to the understanding of "hidden meanings," they gather momentum and encouragement from more intellectual followers as well, so unpopular has the unconscious become. Yet this refusal to accept any meaning other than the one offered by the manifest content of the song, a refusal which by its nature accepts *double entendre* but rejects true symbolism or unconscious significance, has for many of these followers a rather thinly disguised racist implication. The implication, of course, is that lower-class blacks have no unconscious, no capacity to symbolize, but only the capacity to suggest and allude. Hopefully, no more need be said about this, other than that such a concept is quite beyond belief and only follows from the crisis of critical thought that we are witnessing today.

Yet there is hope — no doubt baffled and puzzled by their own inability to grasp the essence of certain mental processes, critics have, for the most part, kept their hands off *the right to dream;* and thus humanity's most valuable and most fertile mental activity has been spared unwarranted "criticism" and interference. Throughout all, the dream still claims its essential place in the fabric of human life, and retains its unbreakable connection with the necessity of freedom and the demand for total reconstruction of the world according to desire.

The Physician Curing Fantasy (French School, 17th century).

THE DREAM

> When History sleeps, it speaks in
> dreams: on the brow of the sleeping, the
> poem is a constellation of blood. When
> History wakes, image becomes deed, the
> poem is achieved: poetry goes into action.
> — Octavio Paz

It is impossible to discuss the dream simply as a dream. In spite of the fundamental correctness of the psychoanalytic conception of the dream, it is imperative that those aspects or implications of the dream which clearly at this time lie beyond psychoanalysis be given the attention they deserve. I refer, of course, to poetry, to freedom, to the resolution of the contradiction between conscious and unconscious, to the destruction of bourgeois morality, to the total emancipation of humanity. Reality must be transformed from top to bottom:

I had a dream, I had a dream one rainy night. (x2)
I was looking for my baby and you know the sun was
shining bright.
(Elmore James, *The Sun Is Shining*)

Each section of this book has had a specific critical purpose. The themes discussed play a significant part in human life, so much so that *now* — in our discussion of the dream — we find ourselves face to face with the same themes again. It is no accident that they all find themselves associated with dreaming. The dream is a focal point for the aspiration for freedom, and if according to Freud the dream is a wish-fulfillment, I would be the last to deny it.

It was a dream, just a dream I had on my mind. (x2)
And when I woke up, baby, not a thing could I find.

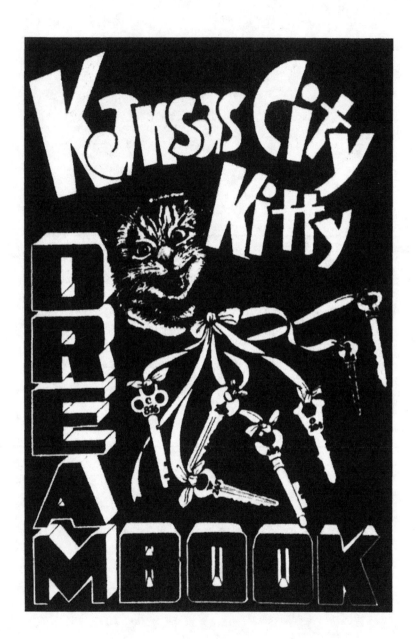

KANSAS CITY KITTY DREAM BOOK

I dreamed I went out with an angel, and had a good time.
I dreamed I was satisfied and nothing to worry my mind.
But it was a dream, etc.
And when I woke up, baby, not an angel could I find.

I dreamed I played policy and played the horses, too.
I dreamed I win so much money I didn't know what to do.
But it was a dream, etc.
And when I woke up, baby, not a penny could I find.

I dreamed I was married and started a family.
I dreamed I had ten children and they all looked like me.
But it was a dream, etc.
And when I woke up, baby, not a child could I find.
        (Big Bill Broonzy, *Just a Dream*)

There is a hint in the blues that the dream has a crucial function:

Little Laura was a gal (she was) sixteen,
And Jimmy didn't want to listen to her dreams.
Little Laura was a dreamer, dreamed (herself insane).
She's the dreamiest gal, dreamiest gal I ever seen.

Now she dreamed she was going with the man next door.
She dreamed she was kissing (it) all, all over.
She dreamed she was riding (in) a tall man's automobile.
She's the dreamiest gal, dreamiest gal I ever seen.

Now she dreamed she was sitting (in) the grass by the mill.
She dreamed she had taken me from (my) gal on the hill.
Little Laura was a dreamer, most all her dreams fulfilled.
She's the dreamiest gal, dreamiest gal I ever seen.

Now she dreamed I was hugging her close to my breast.
She told Jimmy that much of the dream, but she wouldn't

tell the rest.
Little Laura was a dreamer, she dreamed herself insane.
She's the dreamiest gal, dreamiest gal I ever seen.

Now she dreamed about loving,
  some (from?) kisses on down.
She's the dreamiest gal for miles
  around.
Little Laura was a dreamer,
  most all her dreams come true.
She had a dream all about loving
  and she knows just what to do.
    (Sleepy John Estes,
      Little Laura Blues)

(If) I('d) listen to my baby, when she was telling me her
  dream. (x2)
Lord, everything now, baby, would have been peaches and
  cream.

I had money on the horses, money on one, two, three. (x2)
Now my water got muddy, and my horse run into a tree.

Now when I had money, I had friends and a real good
  home. (x2)
Lord, I done lost my money, and my friends and home is
  gone.

Now if I'd a listened to my mother, Lord, what she said. (x2)
Lord, I would not a been here now, laying in this ol'
  hospital bed.
    (Big Bill Broonzy, *When I Had Money*)

It was left to Freud to enlighten those intellectuals who scoffed at the lower classes for consulting their dream-books. The intellectuals were the fools, for dreams did have meaning — as for the dream-books, they were indeed unscientific, but as Freud (1900:100) suggested, they were one of "those not infrequent cases in which an ancient and jealously held popular belief seems to be nearer the truth than the judgment of the prevalent science of today." Much the same can be said for superstition and magic.

> I had a dream last night, and it filled me full of fright. (x2)
> I dreamed I was in the dance hall where the devil danced at night.
>
> I saw the sweet Mrs. devil standing in her hall. (x2)
> She was out with the devil, (said) she was giving a ball.
>
> She had on a robe that was made of gold. (x2)
> I never seen no devil look so sweet before.
>
> It was a dream, a dream I never had before. (x2)
> I dreamed we all was dancing and put on a great big show.
> (Sippie Wallace, *Devil Dance Blues*)

It was also Freud *(Minutes,* op. cit.) who suggested that the devil represents the personification of the unconscious and repressed instincts. According to Evans (1971:108), "learning music from the devil is a common motif in negro folklore." Once again, we have an irrefutable confirmation of the role of the unconscious. Its specific function in the creation of blues songs cannot be lost from sight. The blues singer may be confirming a segment of psychoanalytic theory when he sings:

> I went to town this morning and bought a new pair of shoes. (x2)
> I didn't do it 'cause I wanted to, done it cause I had the blues.
> (Lightnin' Hopkins, *Got to Move Your Baby*)

But there's a trace of magic there. And it is precisely in magic that we find the poetic means for the transformation of reality.

Going to Louisiana bottoms to get me a hoodoo hand. (x2)
To try to stop the women from taking my man.

The hoodoo told me to get me a black cat bone. (x2)
And "Shake it over their head, they'll leave your man alone."
(Ma Rainey, *Louisiana Hoo Doo Blues*)

Human freedom depends not only on the destruction and restructuring of the economic system, but on the restructuring of the mind. New modes of poetic action, new networks of analogy, new possibilities of expression all help formulate the nature of the supersession of reality, the transformation of everyday life as it encumbers us today, the unfolding and eventual triumph of the marvelous:

A tadpole in the river, hatching underneath of a log. (x2)
He got too old to be a tadpole, he turned into a natural frog.

If a toad-frog had wings, he would be flying all around. (x2)
He would not have his bottom bumpin' thumpin' on the ground.

Everytime I see a toad-frog, Lord, it makes me cry. (x2)
It makes me think about my baby, way she rolls her goo-goo eyes.
(Walter Beasley, *Toad Frog Blues*)

Dreaming remains intimately connected with all of the above-mentioned possibilities, for it is in the dream that we see, once again, the satisfaction of our desires; moreover, in reproducing the gratification of repressed wishes, often we see new possibilities of unrepressed life. If the surrealists and their precursors have been preoccupied with these themes, it would be unjust not to give credit to the blues artists as well. As I wrote earlier (1970a:30), "It is significant that the currents of 19th century French poetry that Tristan Tzara, in 1931, found relevant to surrealist excursion are a fairly accurate description of the content of the blues. Among Tzara's subjects were: phantoms, magic, sexual liberty, dreams, madness, passion, folklore, and real and imaginary voyages." Nothing has changed, least of all the dream.

The blues, like the dream, continues to retain its rights — even if its future is uncertain. We see in it an appeal to close the shutters on a withered concept of virtue and a harsh and oppressive civilization; we see in it a demand for non-repression, elaborated by the images of a capacity for fantasy that has not been crushed. We see in it one of the few modern American poetic voices through which humanity has fiercely fought for, and managed to regain, a semblance of its true dignity.

Notes

[1] We should add here a further item of advice from psychoanalysis regarding the nature of the unconscious. Everything that is unconscious is not necessarily symbolized. Since it is only the symbol that retains universal meaning, there is no way of estimating the unconscious significance of numerous nonsymbolized references in the songs. There are any number of ideas and objects that represent one thing to the unconscious of one person and another thing to the unconscious of another. It is because of this that song-analysis (or dream-analysis) can never proceed past the symbol-interpretation stage without the free associations of the singer (or dreamer).

[2] As a corollary to this view, Róheim (1945:196) suggests that in so far as snakes stand erect, or are thought to, the snake represents the penis,

but in so far as they also swallow things, or beings, they may "typify fantasies and anxieties connected with vagina and uterus."

[3] Regarding whether or not dreams foretell the future, as some dream-books suggest, there is a kernel of truth supported even by psychoanalysis. The issue finds itself further opened by J. W. Dunne's *An Experiment with Time* (1958).

tough times

"Tough times, tough times, and people
don't know what to do."
— Muddy Waters, *Tough Times*

> Music is dangerous.
> —Surrealist expression

WHAT CHANGES HAS THE BLUES UNDERGONE SINCE *BLUES AND THE POETIC SPIRIT* addressed, in 1975, the multitude of social, erotic, and psycho/poetic tensions that formed the dynamic basis of blues and the blues life? Is the blues in trouble, or is it undergoing a great revival? Are its greatest aficionados helping the blues to survive or are they also its greatest enemies? And, finally, are we always talking about the same thing when we talk about the blues? Can it be defined in musical terms only, or do we need to understand its social context to understand its essence?

These questions cannot be broached without a discussion of the current racist and conservative political climate. The increase in police repression and brutality against urban blacks is reminiscent of the worst eras of racist law enforcement, while the black ghetto response has become more violent, stark, and desperate. It is an atmosphere in which the blues statement is made almost obsolete, pushed into obscurity by the sounds of "gangsta rap."

This particular evolution seems an inevitable progression in the attempt to deal with the realities of ghetto life in both a compatible and artistic fashion. That we are dealing with *evolution* is underscored in Robin D. G. Kelley's assertion that blues is the "most significant ancestor" of rap. Rap's major proponents have configured it to deal with the violence of today's culture in ways for which the blues is seemingly unsuited. It is almost as if, among the various impulses that underwent sublimation in the blues' evolution, some have come unwound, released from sublimation to seek a more direct and violent outlet in the forceful rhythms and savage claims of gangsta rap and in the brutal and turbulent activities of daily life itself.

Blues "preserved the function of negation" at a time when other instruments of revolt were unavailable. The age of rap seems to claim that other forces of negation have taken the stage, and the blues — symbolically displaced by the closing of Chicago's Maxwell Street — now enters an age of wandering, searching for a new stage from which it can hone its poetic weapons.[1]

But it bears repeating: This age of wandering takes place in a specific political climate. Racism, reaction, and conservatism have made sweeping inroads into our lives, and the blues, and black culture in general, have felt the pressure of these forces. Rap is a direct artistic response to the domination of conservative politics, and these same political tendencies have affected the blues in diverse ways. As bluesman Sugar Blue remarked, "Has things changed in the last 40 years? Yes, they've gotten worse. . . ."[2]

Worse, indeed! While from another perspective the blues *seems* to be undergoing a *revival,* the very fiber of its being, its most vital center, is rapidly disappearing at the hands of new white performers. While this may apparently have little to do with the United States' swing to the right, a closer look reveals some surprising facts.

One of the most distressing aspects of the contemporary

white blues phenomenon is its silent complicity with the current atmosphere of racism and reaction in the United States. The secret weapon in 1990s racism is the notion that racial discrimination is a thing of the past, and that we have now entered the era of true colorblindness. Defenders of white blues often claim that by refusing to use race as a criterion for anything, they are the ultimate non-racists. But they are really resisting the importance of *consciousness of race* and race matters by blinding themselves to the complexity of racial issues and the anti-black racism that still fuels American life.

In the 1990s, "racial equality" is simply the newest name for the dismantling of civil rights legislation, the end of affirmative action, and the destruction of many of the gains blacks have made in the past four decades.

Colorblindness can also blind us to what is specifically black about the blues. For me, race-specificity is what the blues is all about. If the blues is solely an African American art form, there must be something in the blues that is unique to African Americans. Indeed there is, but it is not an inborn propensity to be able to sing the blues, nor is it a unique bit of genetic code that has an affinity for flatted 3rds, 5ths or 7ths. Rather, what is uniquely black about the blues is a system of reference based on shared experience, in the past and in the present; it is a cultural matter, not a racial or biological one. That shared experience is slavery and its shadow, the subsequent oppression and racism that have been visited upon blacks at the hands of whites. The blues, formed in this crucible stirred and agitated by white racism, was the product of black creativity and genius under the pressure of racism, and as such, a unique cultural achievement. The blues deals with the sorrows, sufferings, and pleasures of humanity as a whole, but its central core of meanings and its style are uniquely black. There are intrinsically black figures, metaphors, and myths that define the blues and the culture from which it sprang, and these characteristics are alien to non-black performance.

Inspired by the works of Sterling Stuckey, Henry Louis Gates and Houston Baker, Samuel Floyd in *The Power of Black Music*[3] isolates these figures, or tropes, as they appear in all forms of black music: hollers, blues, jazz, rhythm and blues, and black classical music. He examines African culture, and he notes the appearance of these devices in U.S. slave culture as well, from Congo Square in New Orleans to the earliest forms of black recorded and non-recorded music. His findings can be divided into three main areas: frame of reference, devices and figures, and patterns of communication. Add to this list the factors of *content* and *consciousness* in these patterns of communication, and we will take the thesis even beyond Floyd's findings.

In his effort to define a black American literary canon, Gates isolates "signifying," which he spells Signifyin(g), as the particular African American frame of reference that permeates black literature. Indeed, signifying *and the blues* are, for Gates, the black tradition's two greatest repositories of theory, encoded linguistically and musically. Gates sees Signifyin(g) and the blues as master tropes for studying black literature. It is Floyd's genius to seize upon this finding as it applies to black music. He is not the first to notice the presence of a type of "signifying" in black music, however. As early as 1956, Marshall Stearns noted that among the West African musical characteristics that could be found in African American music were the "songs of allusion," which invoked *indirection* (the trope of signifying).[4] *Indirection* is also cited by Molefi Kete Asante as a principal African characteristic that appears in black speech.[5]

Signifying is, of course, a form of indirection, but a special form of indirection. It is a black double-voicedness,[6] a form of "figurative, implicative speech," that serves as a way of saying one thing and meaning another.[7] If this sounds like signifying has been broadened beyond its common usage — playing the dozens and other verbal games and assaults — we must point out that signifying is *an entire style of language use,* a style that defines and is defined by the black (speech) community.[8]

There are other indigenous characteristics of black music. Call-and-response, the life blood of African American performer/audience dynamics, and related devices like cries, calls, and hollers, are all derived from African performance practices that survived in the United States under slavery. These characteristics, together with polyrhythms, lyricism, and a tendency to indirection are all *essential* characteristics of African American performance.[9]

This lyricism is significant beyond the content of the lyrics themselves. For while meaning may be carried by the manifest or latent content of the lyrics, the voice and the manner in which the lyrics are delivered carries a meaning of its own. "Some lexical items cannot be powerful, until they are powerfully spoken."[10] Thus, whether or not a song is a blues is determined by the *manner* in which the song is sung. Whatever Bessie Smith sang automatically became a blues — while such performances as *101 Strings Play the Blues* are ridiculous.

Black performance styles embody black cultural values, and these values are not so much inherent in the music as they are produced by "people in their relationships with the music,"[11] and by the performers and their audience during the act of musical performance. One of the values circulated and exchanged is the value of certain myths. "Myth is most pervasive as a mythoform, the all-encompassing deep generator of ideas and concepts in our living relationship with our peers, friends, and ancestors. A productive force, it creates discourse forms that enable speakers to use cultural sources effectively."[12] The myths of which we speak are not universal, but represent the African American response to a historical moment.[13] For some, the blues itself is such a myth, or ritual. According to Julio Finn, brother of bluesman Billy Boy Arnold, "The blues is the *cultural memorial of slavery,* a musical memoir commemorating the history of blacks in the United States" [emphasis added].[14]

But on another level the blues contains or exalts myths of its own. One such is the myth of Stagolee, another is John Henry, another is the devil at the Crossroads. Stagolee is an ideal illus-tration, for thanks to Lloyd Price's crossover version of the famous folk song, many listeners who have little knowledge of the blues have nonetheless heard of Stagolee. Yet at its origins, Stagolee is not simply a song about a barroom shooting. Rather, it is a prototypical myth of the radical and the rebel, embodying in his very existence and survival the impulse to challenge authority. As Furry Lewis sang, and as the woman told the sher-iff, "You want to arrest old Stagolee, you better go someplace else." Stagolee seems to personify reckless violence, yet he is a hero, because his violent nature is seen as a "thorn in the side of white, hypocritical government."[15]

Furthermore, the mythoform of Stagolee is operative throughout the blues, even when the name is not spoken. The explanatory power of myth is by no means lost when it ceases to operate consciously. Indeed, "it is precisely because these "deep utterances" operate at unconscious levels that they main-tain our symbolic life at a conscious level. . . . The artists or speaker who uses these myths may never call explicitly upon the names John Henry or Stagolee to express the truth of the myth. However, the myth is so implicit in the culture that its use is impossible to avoid if one engages in any type of discourse."[16]

Another mythic figure in black life is the devil, and he appears in the blues in many guises. I devoted a full-length study to blues singer Peetie Wheatstraw,[17] who called himself the Devil's Son-in-Law and The High Sheriff of Hell, and Robert Johnson's fabled relationship with the devil has become almost public knowledge. Only slightly less known is Tommy Johnson's insistence that he learned to play the guitar from the devil, who met him at a lonely and deserted crossroads at midnight, tuned his guitar for him, and handed it back to him. All three of these legends derive from the African figure Esu, the Trickster, but this is not to suggest that all African Americans believe in either Esu or the devil. I think Samuel Floyd said it best when he noted that these legends are so important to black Americans, so intrinsic to their survival, that they treasured these memories and behaved as if the legends were true, long after they stopped believing in them.[18]

The blues is a language of the richest complexity. For it to speak at its full power, black musicans must speak with black audiences, audiences who share their emotional and cultural background and who will therefore be open to the deepest and broadest comprehension of the messages the blues transmits. This not only means that songs carry latent and manifest meaning, evoking the mythic power of Stagolee and the devil, on conscious and unconscious levels, but that the performers and audience are in tune with those myths as they have been molded in the fire of the imagination of an oppressed people. This is the blues as the product of black creativity and genius forged under the pressure of racism.

It is more than ironic that whites fail to grasp that what they are appropriating is a music that blacks created not only as an entertainment, but as an eloquent and coded protest against white rule and appropriation. They seize the body's limbs and leave the heart behind.

Worse, some of "white blues" current performers were inspired by the antics of the popular white comedians Dan Ackroyd and John Belushi doing their characterization of Jake and Elwood Blues, The Blues Brothers. The LP and the movie ignited a trend — based on a *joke*, mind you — that went beyond the wildest dreams of any of the participants. For many new white performers the notion of the blues' "black heritage" is indeed a mystery; the only "heritage" they know is sun glasses, black suits and fedoras, which have become one of the classic new white blues uniforms. This commercial exploitation helps to explain why the blues has become isolated from black culture. They rarely read black critics or seek out the black point of view on any subject, and they lack interest in black thought, black ideas, black arts, or black speech, i.e., black culture in general.

Let me cite a very plain example of what gets lost in the

translation, from *Promised Land* by Chuck Berry. In his attempt to cross the U.S. to the "promised land" of the West Coast, the protagonist of Berry's song is on a Greyhound bus that breaks down and strands the passengers in Birmingham. He buys a ticket "across Mississippi, clean," that is, nonstop. This is obviously a form of "deep utterance," that resonates back through Robert Johnson's "Dark gon' catch me here," and farther, on through the Scottsboro case, finally dead-ending against the branches of a lynching tree. For a black man to be stranded somewhere in the deep South was bad enough, but in Mississippi? Stranded? Never! Thus, Berry's protagonist bought a ticket that would take him from Birmingham, Alabama, entirely across Mississippi without stopping until he crossed the state's western border.

Yet listen to the song as performed by Elvis Presley and note how empty the line is about "across Mississippi, clean." All the deepest meanings are gone, leaving only the reference to a nonstop trip across an entire state. This is an obvious example from a rock 'n' roll song, but white blues constantly manifests a hollowness that is scattered throughout almost every performance.

Another example: Stagolee is the mythic presence that pervades nearly all the blues of violence: Howlin' Wolf's version of *44 Blues,* Lightnin' Hopkins *Shotgun Blues,* Skip James' *22-20 Blues* and Georgia Tom's *Six-Shooter Blues* are typical examples. The myth does not have to be mentioned or even be present in consciousness for it to be a determining factor, for its truth is implicit in the discourse of the culture itself, a culture where violence has derived from the tyranny of slavery and post-slavery oppression and discrimination. Yet when white performers sing these violent songs, the lack of cultural context leaves only a mockery of empty boasting.[19]

The principal thesis of *Blues and the Poetic Spirit* is that the blues is a music that signifies the rebellion of the spirit, a body of song that achieves poetry by its insistent revolt and demand for liberation. Had it not been created through the genius of an oppressed people, its language and speech would not have contained the same demands. Before the blues revival of the 1960s, it was taken for granted that blues contained an eloquent protest, but during the blues revival, professional pessimists, hailing themselves as realists, declared that such protest could not be detected in blues lyrics.[20] This, after decades of scholarship had uncovered the hidden meanings and the rebelliousness "coded" in spirituals, and decades after these findings were totally accepted!

Why not the blues? Why was its content not subject to the same analysis and the same revelations? For many academics, resistance to psychoanalysis was the big problem. These blues fans worked and studied in various university departments: anthropology, American studies, music, etc. Folklore departments were few and far between. One notion held in common was a hostility to psychoanalytic thinking and a distrust of any form of interpretation that claimed to assess unconscious meanings and their symbolic expression.

Trained in a fierce and dogged literalism, where imagination played an exceedingly minor role compared to persistence and discipline, it was difficult for them to believe that blues singers might be singing about something other than the obvious. Thus, academic observers were destined — condemned from the start — to miss any hidden meanings the blues had to offer.

There are other, more important reasons, however, and some of them are unpleasant to behold. Blues research during the revival years was carried on, in the minds of the field workers, in an atmosphere of cordiality and cooperation. Yet 98% of these field workers were white. Perhaps it was pride that made it impossible for them to admit to themselves that their black compatriots were holding something back and held deep secrets that were still beyond sharing with whites. For modern researchers to ignore the possiblity of protest in blues also allowed them to think of blues as a music of accommodation, a more comfortable thought than the notion that it might be a music of resistance and that they might be working with singers who considered them the enemy! Let us speak openly. Often the whites were in positions of power: agents, A-and-R men, label owners, magazine editors and writers. Did they really expect black artists to speak to them honestly about their feelings for whites in general and for them in particular? An example will clarify this. In the famous documentary recording, *Blues in the Mississippi Night*, Memphis Slim, Big Bill Broonzy and Sonny Boy Williamson talked to Alan Lomax with unusual candor about the blues and life for African Americans in the South. When Lomax played back the recording of their discussion, triumphant about the candor he had elicited, "they were terrified. They begged me never to tell anyone they had made the recordings."[21] The recordings were issued over a decade later, with the principals identified only by pseudonyms. Thus, while blacks were understandably fearful of telling a white man their true feelings about whites, they were able to make an exception for Alan Lomax. As we know, this was an exception Blind Willie McTell refused to make for John Lomax, Alan's father, when he tried to convince McTell to record for him some protest songs for the Library of Congress.[22] The elder Lomax's experience was the more common one, it seems, but Alan's was hardly the only case of the curtain of fear being drawn aside.

At the time, Lawrence Gellert's important field recordings had yet to be released, but now they have been: Here are acoustic guitar blues, recorded in the 1920s, rife with protest themes.[23] Gellert had also recorded hundreds of work and prison songs with overt protest themes.[24] But Gellert was a white man with a black wife and a trusted member of the black community, unlike the field researchers of the 1960s and later. Many of the Gellert-collected songs were published in the mid-1930s, in books[25] and in *New Masses*, but most observers refused to see that the recorded blues were the coded versions of these same pieces, coded just as the spirituals were. Without diagrams, modern critics were lost.

Now we have more diagrams, supplied by the singers themselves. Some of them date back to the 1940s. Memphis Slim told Alan Lomax, "[B]lues is a kind of a revenge. You know you wanta say something . . . you wanta signifyin' like — that's the blues. . . . [W]e-all fellers, we had a hard time in life an' like that, and things we couldn't say or do, so we sign it, I mean we sing." Slim goes on to talk about a friend who couldn't talk back to his work captain, but still had to work: "[S]o it give him the blues, and he can't speak his mind. So he made a song of it, he sang it. Still, *he was signifying and getting his revenge through songs*" [emphasis added].[26] What plainer confirmation of the theory of blues as a signifying, coded language could we ask for?

More recently, Little Willie Foster remarked that the lyric, "My baby mistreats me," often meant "My boss mistreats me," while Willie Cobb remarked that "My baby walked away" was his way of singing, "My white lawyer walked away."[27]

Singers have become more vocal about the amount of money and attention devoted to white performers of black music, and point out that white blues isn't really the blues.

Here's Buddy Guy's *Don't Tell Me About the Blues,* from his 1995 CD, *Slippin' In*[28]

Yeah, you down-and-dirty blues man,
(*spoken:* looka here)
You play blues on blues guitar
I'm telling it to the news, man,
As far as blues goes, you're a star
I'll admit you're getting down there,
But I'm down much deeper than you are.

Yeah, you sing those songs of sorrow,
But to me you just don't sound real.
You say you're down enough to borrow,
I must be down enough to steal.
Now, the blues ain't what you're singing,
The blues is what I feel.

You tell me your love-light is dimming,
And how your old lady cheats,
You go back stage with other women,
While I go back out on the street.
Well, you know that you're a winner,
And you tell me you were born to lose,
But please, please, please
Don't tell me about the blues.

You're telling like your barefoots
And you're wearing those $100 shoes.
Yeah, you can shuck and jive me all you wanta,
But please, please don't tell me about the blues.
etc.

Guy's feelings here were a surprise to many white blues players because they believed that only white critics felt this way, not
black artists. "Didn't Muddy hire Bob Margolin?" they ask. Well,
yes he did, for whatever reasons. If I had to guess why, I would
say Muddy hired him because he thought having a white band
member would be consistent with the fact that most of his audience was, by then, white. But this is only a guess. Nonetheless,
this is the same Muddy Waters who commented on white blues
musicians: "I think they're great people, but they're not blues
players." [29] He also remarked, "They got all these white kids
now. Some of them can play *good* blues. They play so much, run
a ring around you playin' guitar, but they cannot vocal like the
black man." [30] Muddy may even have been signifying on the
white preoccupation with flashiness when he said "run a ring
around you," but who knows? Indeed, Muddy certainly hadn't
forgotten that so many blues-singing blacks were blues *singers*
who often accompanied themselves, sometimes with stunning
guitar, harp, or piano styles. The occasional weak-voiced singer
usually had a superlative instrumental technique to compensate.
Whites, on the other hand, tended to be flashy instrumentalists

with inappropriate blues voices, fetishizing fast and ostentatious guitar techniques.[31]

Here is young Chicago blues singer/guitarist Tré Hardiman: "They take everything from us. Give us the blues. . . . The only definition of blues artist that should be in the *American Heritage Dictionary* is black, male or female, poverty-stricken, livin' and singin' and eatin' the blues for a livin'."[32]

Sugar Blue was more outspoken in a *Down Beat* interview: "The American would rather listen to a white English rock group playing indigenous American music. I think that speaks very badly of American mores, of their social, racial and economic values, but that is America. . . . They can listen to the blues from Elvis . . . but they couldn't listen to that from the people who wrote it. What's wrong with it is the fact you had to hear it as a fucking pale echo of what it really is. . . . That's what's still wrong in this country. . . . It's about what this [the color of my skin] makes me have to live in this world. The experience of that lifestyle permeates this music, and if you have not lived it, you cannot fuckin' play it."[33]

Is Sugar Blue's commentary unusual? Hardly. Julio Finn wrote that the problem of the white blues performers was that "they can never be *bluespeople* . . . because the blues is not something they *live* but something they *do* — which makes all the difference in the world. What distinguishes the bluesperson from the blues performer is cultural-racial make-up, which can only be inherited by a descendant of an ex-American slave. . . .

"The blues is . . . the product of a special kind of inhumanity one people suffered at the hands of another. The outcome has been an art form so deeply imbued with the stamp of that experience that it is inseparable from the people from whom it springs."[34] Finn's angry voice is a far cry from the white blues performers who feel they are taking part in "a great cultural interchange where the American melting-pot once again allows people of all races to share their cultures."[35] No! For blacks, this is an ironic and mean-spirited notion that covers up the salient fact of white appropriation.

Of course, blues isn't the only form of black music subject to white appropriation. Jazz composer and bassist Charles Mingus commented on jazz, "It's the American Negro's tradition, it's his music. . . . You had your Shakespeare, and Marx, and Einstein, and Jesus Christ and Guy Lombardo but we came up with jazz, don't forget it, and all the pop music in the world today is from that primary cause."[36] Thelonious Monk, speaking of white dance bands, said they "had carried off the healthiest child of Negro music, and starved it of its spirit until its parents no longer recognized it."[37] As befitting a poet, Langston Hughes was more succinct, "You've taken my blues and gone."[38]

Notes

[1] Kelley, Robin D. G. *Race Rebels. Culture, Politics, and the Black Working Class*. NY: Free Press, 1994. For related material, see George, Nelson. *The Death of Rhythm and Blues*. NY: Pantheon, 1988.

[2] Sugar Blue, quoted in Helland, Dave. "Harp to Harp. Junior Wells and Sugar Blue" in *Down Beat*, October, 1995, p. 27.

[3] Floyd, Samuel. *The Power of Black Music*. NY: Oxford, 1995.

[4] Stearns, Marshall. *The Story of Jazz*. NY: Oxford, 1956, p. 13.

[5] Asante, Molefi Kete. *The Afrocentric Idea*. Philadelphia: Temple University Press, 1987.

[6] Gates, Henry Louis, Jr. *The Signifying Monkey*. NY: Oxford, 1988, p. 56.

[7] Floyd, p. 95.

[8] Gates, p. 81.

[9] See, for example, Asante, p. 48.

[10] Asante, p. 48.

[11] Floyd, p. 275.

[12] Asante, p. 96.

[13] Asante, p. 98.

[14] Finn, Julio. *The Bluesman*. London: Quartet Books, 1986, p. 230.

[15] Asante, p. 107.

[16] Asante, pp. 96, 107–8.

17 Garon, Paul. *The Devil's Son-in-Law. The Story of Peetie Wheatstraw and His Songs.* London: Studio Vista, 1971.

18 Floyd, p. 74.

19 This same point is made about rock and roll by Martha Bayles in *Hole in Our Soul. The Loss of Beauty and Meaning in American Popular Music.* NY: Free Press, 1994, p. 200. I also know of one case where the black idiom was so unfamiliar to a "white blues" performer that he had to ask his friends whether or not the song he was about to play was offensive.

20 See, for example, Titon, Jeff. *Early Downhome Blues.* Urbana: University of Illinois Press, 1977, pp. 190-191, and elsewhere, or the Introduction to Peter Guralnick's *Feel Like Going Home.* NY: Outerbridge and Dienstfrey, 1971, pp. 22-23.

21 Lomax, Alan. "Blues in the Mississippi Night — The Story of the Recording" *Blues in the Mississippi Night.* Salem: Rykodisc, 1990 (orig. 1947), p. 11.

22 John Lomax interviewing McTell may be heard on *Blind Willie McTell: 1940. The Legendary Library of Congress Session.* Arlington: Melodeon Records, n.d.

23 Gellert, Lawrence, comp. *Nobody Knows My Name. Blues from South Carolina and Georgia.* Crawley, West Sussex, Interstate Music/Heritage Records.

24 Gellert, Lawrence, comp. *Negro Songs of Protest.* Somerville, MA: Rounder Records, and Gellert, Lawrence, comp. *Cap'n You're So Mean.* Somerville, MA: Rounder Records.

25 Gellert, Lawrence, comp. *Negro Songs of Protest.* NY: American Music League, 1936, and Gellert, Lawrence, comp. *"Me and My Captain" (Chain Gangs).* NY: Hours, 1939.

26 Memphis Slim, *Blues in the Mississippi Night.* Rykodisc, 1990.

27 Willie Cobb's testimony was a personal remark to Jim O'Neal.

28 Guy, Buddy. *Don't Tell Me About the Blues,* on *Slippin' In.* Silvertone Records [CD], 1995.

29 Guralnick, p. 62.

30 Palmer, Robert. *Deep Blues.* NY: Viking, 1981, p. 260.

31 Bayles, p. 192.

32 Hardiman, Tré, quoted in Steven Sharp, "Chicago Special," in *Living Blues* 123. September/October 1995, p. 38.

[33] Helland, Dave. "Harp to Harp, Junior Wells and Sugar Blue," in *Down Beat*, October 1995, pp. 27-28.

[34] Finn, pp. 229-230.

[35] Anonymous internet message to the author.

[36] Mingus, Charles, quoted in Alfred B. Pasteur and Ivory L. Toldson, *The Roots of Soul. The Psychology of Black Expressiveness*. Garden City: Anchor Press/Doubleday, 1982, p. 137.

[37] Monk, Thelonious, quoted in "The Loneliest Monk," in *Time*, June 20, 1964, p. 86.

[38] Hughes, Langston. "Note on Commercial Theatre," in *Selected Poems of Langston Hughes*. NY: Vintage, 1990, p. 190.

appendix:
surrealism and black music

> I chose surrealism when I was very young. . . .
> I sensed in it a camaraderie that I found also in jazz.
>
> — Ted Joans

SURREALISM IS SO PERSISTENTLY MISUNDERSTOOD, ESPECIALLY IN the English-speaking world (and above all by the academic "specialists" in surrealism, with few exceptions), that a brief digression seems called for here to specify in somewhat greater detail the fundamental premises of the present work. On the poetic plane surrealism constitutes the most far-reaching revolution of modern times — even its enemies are often willing to concede this point. And because the surrealist conception of poetry goes far beyond the poem, exceeding every alienated category and implying the thoroughgoing poetic transformation of everyday life (in accord with Lautréamont's dictum, "Poetry must be made by all," which the surrealists make theirs), the surrealist revolution increasingly extends its hegemony over all problems relating to human expression. In English-speaking countries most developed industrially and to some extent for that very reason most backward poetically — surrealism has only recently found its voice in a sustained organized activity. The movement's greatest theoretical works by André Breton, Benjamin Péret, René Crevel, Pierre Mabille, Vincent Bounoure, Karel Teige, Vratislav Effenberger, Gherasim Luca et al. — remain largely untranslated and unknown; consequently, poetic "problems" in English are generally discussed either within an outmoded and decrepit "symbolist" or "imagist" framework or in the spirit of a completely incoherent and individualistic eclecticism: "every man for himself."

I would like briefly to take up the problem of *surrealism and music,* and especially surrealism and black music, which has been totally obfuscated by critics of every persuasion.

The founder of surrealism André Breton, wrote in *Surrealism and Painting* (1928) that musical expression was "the most deeply confusing of all forms." Similar critical pronouncements are not infrequent in the writings of other surrealists of the first generation. It is well known, too, that there have been few surrealist composers. The surrealists have always disdained the symbolists' prostration before a deified Music, and have even championed the Italian painter Georgio di Chirico's watchword: "No music!" Perhaps the most detailed surrealist examination of music, particularly as it relates to affective states, is the Belgian Paul Nougé's 1929 *Conference de Charleroi,* available in English under the title *Music Is Dangerous.*

Literary gossips and critical rumor mongers have added their own confusion to the discussion of the apparent surrealist antipathy to music, viewing it (in keeping with the narrow-mindedness typical of critics) as a purely idiosyncratic phenomenon. Matthew Josephson, for example, in his very unreliable *Life Among the Surrealists,* considers the surrealists' opposition to music a mere prejudice of Breton's compulsorily shared by the other surrealists. Fortunately Josephson's habitual inaccuracies and his ill-concealed hostility to surrealism generally and to Breton particularly are so blatant that it is unnecessary to stoop to refute his allegations here. But Josephson's abject anecdotal oversimplifications have the virtue of a sort of candor, even if it is the dubious candor of a pensioned stoolpigeon. Far worse, in terms of clarity, is the ridiculous article "Surrealism and Music" by Nicolas Slonimsky, appropriately published in the antisurrealist issue of the U.S. art magazine *Artforum* (September 1966). Slonimsky proposes the most trivial "definition" of surrealism — so that it includes any little deviation from the ordinary and proceeds to enumerate a vast array of "surrealist" composers and musicians who, of course, have absolutely nothing to do with surrealism. To critical noisemakers of this sort one can hardly help but prefer silence.

The original surrealists' hostility to music focused on the music at hand — above all French salon music and the "light Classical" style that typified the 1920s' petty-bourgeois insistence on moderation at all costs. With few exceptions the early surrealists also rejected the "avant-garde" experiments of composers such as Erik Satie, which they regarded as a dead-end. Moreover, the literary charlatan Jean Cocteau (a "false poet," as Breton described him) was widely recognized as the "champion" of Music throughout the French literary/artistic milieu: this alone sufficed to provoke the surrealists' aversion. But it should he emphasized that there was no rigid "party line" on the question of music. The Belgian E.L.T. Mesens abandoned writing music ("for moral reasons") at the time of his adherence to surrealism, but nonetheless remained friendly with Erik Satie and even wrote about him. Breton always recognized that his indifference to music was largely a matter of individual temperament, though he remarked that such indifference was shared by a great majority of French poets throughout the Romantic and post-Romantic era. But I am told that Breton was fond of certain popular French theatrical songs, music roughly comparable to the librettoes of Gilbert & Sullivan. The surrealist poet Paul Eluard included not a few lines from French popular songs in his poems. It is also interesting that Benjamin Péret's first wife, Elsie Houston, edited an extensive anthology of Brazilian folksongs.

Some of these "exceptions" give us an important clue that permits us already to see the possible surrealist interest in the blues: there is a distinction between music, as such, and song. And in the one article that Breton devoted to the subject of music ("Silence Is Golden, 1944") he emphasized the crucial importance of song as a synthesis of music and poetry. In this important and suggestive article, Breton (recalling Hegel's classification of the arts in which music follows poetry but precedes the plastic arts) declares boldly: ". . . I am convinced that the antagonism which exists between poetry and music (apparently affecting poets much more than it does musicians), and which for some ears seems to have reached its height today, should not be fruitlessly deplored but, on the contrary, should be interpreted as an indication of the *necessity for the recasting* of certain principles of the two arts." And he continues: ". . . I am merely taking up again one of my favorite themes: that we should never miss an opportunity 'to take by the horns' all the antinomies presented by modern thought, in order first to protect ourselves from them, then to tame and overcome them. . . . Music and poetry have everything to lose by not recognizing a common origin and common end *in song,* by letting the mouth of Orpheus get farther every day from the lyre of Thrace. Poet and musician will degenerate if they persist in acting as though these two forces were never to be brought together again."

It could be said that in music the first surrealists found themselves especially interested in extra-musical qualities, just as in painting they insisted on extra-painterly qualities. It hardly need be said that the blues in particular, and American black music generally, is characterized by numerous extra-musical qualities: for the blues is primarily sung and, like jazz, involves an entire comportment, thoroughly rooted in the violent exigencies of the black U.S. proletariat throughout the post-slavery epoch, and sufficient to place it well beyond the categories of any mere "aesthetics" of music.

No attempt has been made yet by scholars to trace the surrealists' interest in American black music — in fact, the official pretension is that no such interest has existed. It is therefore entirely in order here to survey at least some of the evidence, scattered throughout various old texts, obscure chronicles and memoirs. It is my contention that these early echoes of American black music among the surrealists offer invaluable guidelines for viewing the whole question of the blues in an entirely new light. Moreover, these anticipatory echoes also offer many provocative suggestions for further research. I should add that the following notes by no means indicate any search for mere exegetical justification for the present study, but rather a background against which one can better perceive the specific orientation of this work. "In matters of revolt," as Breton wrote, "one should not need ancestors." But while the decisive encounter of surrealism and black music today can be regarded as inevitable, it is nonetheless of considerable theoretical interest to trace the earlier intimations of this encounter the various steps along the road which brought us to our present position.

Certainly poignant, even if ambiguous, is Breton's remark in the invocation to the Orient in the last paragraph of his 1924 *Introduction to the Discourse on the Paucity of Reality:* "In the flow of a phrase as well as in the mysterious wind of jazz, reveal to me your plans for the coming revolutions."

A similarly enticing early reference is that of Ernest Gengenbach (1926), a young man who renounced the priesthood when he discovered surrealism at the very moment that he was contemplating suicide, and who wrote in one of his letters published in the surrealists' journal *La Révolution Surréaliste:* "I have found no solution, no escape, no pragmatism that is acceptable. There remains my faith in Christ, cigarettes, and the jazz records I love — *Tea For Two, Yearning* — and above all there remains *surrealism.*"

André Thirion, who participated in surrealism in the late 1920s and early 1930s, published his lengthy autobiography in 1972, a work useful mostly for its reportage on the surrealists' everyday life. Aside from repeated acknowledgements of his own liking for jazz in those days, Thirion also notes, in passing, that the writer Marcel Duhamel left his large collection of American black music records at the house on the Rue du Chateau, for Thirion lived there with the surrealists Tanguy, the Prévert brothers, their girlfriends, and a constantly revolving network of surrealist visitors. This was in fact one of the principal points of rendezvous for the Paris Surrealist Group in those days. Much later Breton (1952) commented that "surrealism never showed such an organic unity or experienced a greater effervescence than at this period. . . . Absolute non-conformism, total irreverence and also the greatest high spirits reigned at those reunions of ours which were held in the old house in the Rue du Chateau." It is certainly not far-fetched to suggest that this exalted atmosphere was at least in part stimulated by the blues and jazz records which Duhamel left his friends.

In his own memoir of his surrealist days Michel Leiris (1946) wrote, even more strikingly than Thirion: "In the great period of license that followed the hostilities [i.e., World War II] jazz was a sign of allegiance, an orgiastic tribute to the colors of the moment. . . . Swept along by violent bursts of topical energy," Leiris continues, jazz was able "to express quite completely the state of mind of at least some of that generation: a more or less conscious demoralization born of the war . . . an abandonment to the animal joy of experiencing the influence of a modern rhythm, an underlying aspiration to a new life in which more room would be made for the impassioned frankness we inarticulately longed for." Surrealist filmmaker Luis Buñuel was also passionately attracted to black music, and mentions it often in his autobiography, *My Last Sigh*.

It is impossible to chronicle here every surrealist reference to black music; it will suffice to give a few more examples: the surrealist poet Robert Desnos was for a time a disc jockey on a Paris jazz radio program; one of Philippe Soupault's poems is titled "Ragtime"; the first gallery in Amsterdam to exhibit surrealist paintings was also the first place there to feature American black recordings; Karel Teige, in a text written in 1922 (in the following decade Teige would be the leading theorist of surrealism in Czechoslovakia), wrote rapturously of jazz in connection with the cinema. Still less known, but no less intriguing, is the position of the black Martiniquan surrealists Etienne Léro and Réne Ménil who, in association with several comrades also from Martinique, published a single issue of a black surrealist journal, *Légitime Defense,* in 1932. René Ménil concludes an article therein with this unequivocal statement, which amounts to a veritable *programme:* "It is the task of the black West Indian to recognize first of all his own passions and to express only himself, to take . . . the road of dream and of poetry." On this road, Ménil continues, the black West Indian will encounter "fantastic images," such as African sculptures, as well as the "poems, stories and jazz of the American Negroes and the work of some French writers (Lautréamont, Rimbaud, Apollinaire, Jarry, Reverdy, the dadas, the surrealists) who . . . by means of the powers of passion and of dream, have conquered the freshness of Africa."

Ménil's remarks raise another aspect of the surrealist interest in the blues. Surrealism embodies a merciless critique of Western civilization, of European values and ideologies. The surrealists have always defended the genius of non-European cultures — the American Indians, Asia, Oceania, the Caribbean, Africa — in which they found (and continue to find) forms of human expression that are fresher and less accommodative to the structures of individual and social repression. The surrealists recognize confirmations and reinforcements of their own perspectives in the magisterial carvings of the Eskimos, of the woodcarvers of New Ireland or the Northwest Coast Indians of the U.S., the pre-Columbian civilizations of Mexico and Central America, to which many surrealists have devoted very important studies. It follows that the surrealists' sympathetic attention could hardly fail to have been attracted by the vibrant and inspired music created by the American blacks, a music which not only recalls African rhythms and chants, but which is also an impassioned revolt against the white bourgeois "American way of life."

The significance of African origins was touched on by the Austrian surrealist painter Wolfgang Paalen in a brilliant article "On the Meaning of Cubism Today, 1944." Discussing the spatial/temporal dislocation in the cubist paintings of Picasso and Braque, Paalen observed: ". . . I was overwhelmed by an almost ritual power of incantation, by a syncopated rhythm which irresistibly evoked jazz. . . . Rhythms are not arbitrary. Jazz has its roots in the African tom-tom. A tom-tom that I once thought I heard in a lecture-hall where a documentary film on X-ray was being shown. What I confused with the beating of the ageless drum was in actuality the proportionately amplified sound of a greatly magnified human heart. And the beating of the heart-drum is found again in the plastic cadence of the axe blows which liberated the powerful cubes of Negro sculpture that inspired the beating of cubist space. Against a contemporary intellectuality given over to its pretension of being the accountant of the universe, it was the beating of revolt of the new cosmic sense."

The echo from Africa is also insisted on by the Spanish poet Federico García Lorca, who, though never a formal adherent of surrealism, was very close to the movement in the years immediately preceding his murder by Franco's fascists in Spain in 1936. It is probably not a mere coincidence that his most surrealist work is also the work most permeated with the influence of black America: *Poet In New York,* the poetic record of Lorca's voyage to the New World which is evidently the first major surrealist work to bear the unmistakable influence of American black music. In a letter written at the same time as this book, Lorca wrote in 1930: ". . . the sad folk of Africa move in a limbo, adrift in their American setting. The Jews. And the Syrians. And the Negroes. Above all, the Negroes! For the spiritual axis of

America has been shaped by their sadness. The Negro, living close to pure human nature, and other forces of Nature. The Negro spilling music out of his pockets. Apart from the art of the Negro, the United States has nothing to show but machines and automatons."

With the later generation of surrealists the examples of repercussions of black music multiply greatly. It was the Chilean painter Roberto Matta (like many of the surrealists, exiled in New York during World War II) who introduced the surrealists in Paris to the bebop records of Charlie Parker, Thelonious Monk, Dizzy Gillespie and others, which created a sensation among the younger adherents to the movement, as well as some of the elder members: a 1951 painting by Victor Brauner, for example, is titled "Thelonious Monk." Claude Tarnaud's book *La Forme Reflechie* concludes with three prose poems, titled "Miles Davis," "Thelonious Monk" and "Max Roach." A later work of Tarnaud's is dedicated to Monk. Another of the leading figures of postwar surrealism, Gérard Legrand, wrote a book in 1953 titled *Puissances du jazz (Powers of Jazz),* and jazz influences are evident in his later works (his poem "Thanks for the Sphinx" carries the epigraph: "featuring Johnny Hodges"). It is also interesting to note that in his Preface to Breton's *Poésie et autre,* which Legrand edited, he compares Breton's "stance" to that of certain jazz tenor saxophonists: Coleman Hawkins, John Coltrane. Most of the younger surrealists in France, Czechoslovakia, Denmark, Holland, Sweden, England, Australia, Puerto Rico, Brazil and elsewhere have indicated their marked affinity for the revolutionary currents in jazz. If they are less familiar with the blues,[1] it is largely because of the notorious "language barrier." For the blues involves lyrics, lyrics that are not always easily understood even by whites whose native language is English.

It is thus only fitting that this first detailed exploration of the whole range of the blues from the surrealist point of view should be by one whose native language is the language of nearly all the blues. Among the surrealists in the U.S., the blues (and black music generally) has long been a major source of inspiration as well as a kind of fraternal reinforcement of the surrealist project. The works of most of the American surrealists are permeated with the spirit of the blues and jazz, which, as has been argued in the preceding pages, is fundamentally allied to the spirit of poetry and the spirit of human liberty and love.

Thus, despite the reservations of a few misinformed critics, the surrealist attitude on this question (as on all questions) is not dogmatic, for surrealism is not a catechism of unchanging theses; it is based on dialectics and analogy. The Belgian surrealist André Souris, who, perhaps more than any other adherent of the movement, was concerned throughout his life with the question of music, said in 1966: "I do not think there is any specific difference, from the surrealist point of view, between the problems posed by poetry, painting, and music." In *Music Is Dangerous* Paul Nougé asks: "Among all the forces capable of bewitching spirit, forces which it must both submit to and revolt against — poetry, painting, spectacles, war, misery, debauchery, revolution, life with its inseparable companion, death — is it possible to refuse music a place among them, perhaps a very important place?" And he adds: ". . . Whether we deal with music or some other human event, spirit is at our mercy and we are, in reality, accountable for it."

Notes

[1] For the record, let us mention the single specific reference to the blues that I have found in an early surrealist source: a passing remark on the "latest blues" in Jacques Rigaut's 1927 text "New York," included in his *Ecrits* (Paris: Gallimard, 1970:44).

afterword

by Franklin Rosemont

THE BLUES IS AT ONCE A WAY OF LIFE, A VARIETY OF MUSIC, A poetic movement, a state of mind, a folkloric tradition, a moral attitude, and even a kind of spontaneous intuitive critical method. Most commentators agree that it somehow repels all efforts to harness it too tightly in any definition. However, this very indefinability, this *many-sided elusiveness*, is itself revealing about its fundamental character, indicating somewhat its tendency toward universality as well as the emotional heights and depths it is capable of reaching, thus situating it inevitably beyond the grasp of mere "prosaic" articulation. The same is true of jazz. The extreme ardor characteristic of both forms and the crucial role played in both by improvisation suggest that they draw more or less naturally on the deepest, most hidden and most powerful sources of inspiration, as if their adepts were initiated into the use of a kind of Afro-American *philosophers' stone* permitting the imagination to take its revenge on everything that gets in its way.

It should not be lost from sight that American black music originated in the culture of the slaves who were systematically deprived of the more "refined" instruments of human expression. All but a few slaves were forbidden to learn to read or write, and they had little opportunity for plastic expression. Even their musical efforts were severely circumscribed; slaveholders who feared the use of drums and other instruments as means of communication between slave assemblies, and hence as tools of insurrection, banned such instruments from the plantations. Thus the spoken word, the chant, and dancing were the only vehicles of creative expression left to the great majority of slaves. The sublimative energies that in different conditions would doubtless have gone into writing, painting, or sculpture, were necessarily concentrated in the naked word and the naked gesture — in the field hollers, work-songs, and their accompanying rhythmic movements — in which gestated the embryo that would eventually emerge as the blues. Black music developed out of, and later side by side with, this vigorous oral poetry combined with dancing, both nourished in the tropical tempest of black magic and the overwhelming desire for freedom. The extreme repressive context of its origins, and its consequent subsumption into itself of the whole gamut of creative impulses, together give the blues its unique intensity and distinctive poetic resonance.

As a living and fertile body of creative expression blues and jazz retain today their boundless integrity and provocative flare. Their role in shaping the modern sensibility is immense and shows every sign of expanding. It should be emphasized, since so many critics pretend not to notice it, that all authentic blues and jazz share a poetically subversive core, an explosive essence of irreconcilable revolt against the shameful limits of an unlivable destiny. Notwithstanding the whimpering objections of a few timid skeptics, this revolt cannot be "assimilated" into the abject mainstream of American bourgeois/Christian culture except by way of dilution and/or outright falsification. The *dark truth* of Afro-American music remains unquestionably *oppositional*. Its implacable Luciferian pride — that is, its aggressive and uncompromising assertion of the omnipotence of desire and the imagination in the face of all resistances — forever provides a stumbling-block for those who would like to exploit it as a mere commercial diversion, a mere form of "entertainment," a mere ruse to keep the cash register ringing. Born in passionate revolt against the unlivable, blues and jazz demand nothing less than a new life.

Most critics regard the blues as a historically demarcated and easily classifiable trend. But the blues people themselves generally conceive their life's work to be "timeless" and outside conventional critical frameworks. Thus Boogie Woogie Red tells us that "blues have been goin' on for centuries and centuries, and the blues was written years and centuries ago — they was always here" (Oliver 1965:25). It is plain that critics and blues people are here not only speaking of different things, but speaking a different language, reflecting their diametrically opposed outlooks on man and the world. Conventional critics, by definition alienated from the process of poetic production, perceive only stale formal categories, sterile stylistic devices, reified structures of classification, and what Nietzsche called "monumental history," in which the dead weight of the past obstructs the free creative play of the living. Those who actually *play* the blues, however, accentuate its *eternal* character, its *living presence,* its *poetic action* on the human condition. Certainly blues singers, like anyone else, respond to temporal and temporary demands; but their central focus, as poets, is always on an infinitely wider field of action from which nothing, in fact, is closed off.

If one of the prerogatives of poetry is its immunity to criticism, poetry itself nonetheless embodies criticism of the most effective and far-reaching kind. In the present study Paul Garon surveys the blues as a form of poetic praxis viewed in the light of actual poetic and psychological experience, and above all from the angle of poetry itself. Author of poetic texts of ruthless humor and delirium,[1] he also has devoted himself through the years to a meticulous study of the whole range of the blues. His familiarity with psychoanalytic literature, moreover, permits him to substantiate his appreciation of the poetic qualities of the blues by adumbrating some aspects of the mental processes involved in the creation of lyrics. To a great extent it was his profound awareness of all that the blues comprehends and implies that led him into the surrealist movement, in which he has participated actively since 1968.

A study of the blues from the surrealist point of view will not fail, in some quarters, to provoke the raising of eyebrows — a defensive tic which serves in this case only to illustrate the extreme poetic backwardness that still characterizes large sectors of the English-speaking world. The fact is that surrealism, since its inception as an organized movement in 1924, has thrown an unsparing light on everything pertaining to human expression in all its forms. Calling into question all previous poetic ends and means (in accord with its fundamental principle of *absolute divergence*) surrealism has unceasingly provided the contemporary seeker of decisive poetic revelations with new and incomparable weapons and instruments of discovery. Its conquests in poetry, painting and cinema have come to be widely acknowledged, even if not widely understood. Less well known but no less important are its illuminating incursions into the domains of primitive art, the art of the "insane," mythology, dreams, play, humor, and the supremely enticing realms of mad love and objective chance.

Thus far, however, the relationship of surrealism to *music* has been episodic and inconclusive. In contrast to their evident hegemony on other planes of expression, the surrealists have had little recourse to music and have had surprisingly little to say about it. That this reticence is not peculiar to surrealism but is in fact a "sign of the times" is indicated by the psychoanalyst/anthropologist George Devereux (1959:194), who observed that both psychological and cultural studies of music "are, on the whole, more disappointing and also much less numerous than are similar studies devoted to the other arts." The founder of surrealism, André Breton, discussed this problem in his article "Silence Is Golden" (1944), in which he emphasized that "we must determine to *unify, reunify* hearing to the same degree that we must determine to *unify, reunify* sight."

And he added, significantly, that "the fusion of the two elements — music and poetry — could only be accomplished at a very high emotional temperature. And it seems to me that it is in the expression of the passion of love that both music and poetry are most likely to reach this supreme point of incandescence."

No one could seriously deny that the blues represents a fusion of music and poetry "accomplished at a very high emotional temperature." And because of its deep concern with all that touches and is touched by love, the blues would seem to provide an excellent point of departure for an exploration along the lines suggested by Breton. While much of the *musical* side of the blues remains relatively inaccessible, inquiry into its specifically *poetic* aspects is more than justified by the dazzling allure of many blues lyrics. There is reason to expect that this poetic approach will ultimately assist in the clarification of musical factors as well.

On the poetic plane the blues singers can be considered "naive" in the sense that one speaks of "naive" painters: self-taught artists completely outside prevailing aesthetic preoccupations. Their perceptions, and therefore their presentations, are for that very reason often much fresher and livelier, unbiased and unblemished by the morbid ideological contortions of more "educated" creators. It sometimes is argued that this "naive" or "primitive" quality confines the blues irremediably to "traditional" content and impedes all attempts at originality. The splendid lyrics quoted throughout this book amply give the lie to such pretensions. If the blues singers choose not to sing of the Pyramids or the Eiffel Tower — if they remain ignorant of, or indifferent to, the ideological clashes and confusions of bourgeois culture — the reasons are plain. Not the least of these reasons, however, is that other and greater wonders have caught their eyes, wonders that continue to glisten temptingly through the starlit darkness: the unsurpassable wonders of the erotic embrace, the quest for the Golden Fleece of life's most radiant moments, the irresistible enchantments of the night, the inexhaustible exaltation of freedom. It is the blues' "naive" quality that makes it also defiantly *utopian,* in the best sense of the word, imaginatively foreshadowing a happier world.

The revaluation of the blues will contribute to the revaluation of all poetic values by helping us to view the whole development of English-language poetry from a new perspective. Everyone whose knowledge of the blues and poetry is firsthand will know what I mean when I say that William Langland's *Vision of Piers Plowman,* for example, or the works of Thomas Chatterton and William Blake and Emily Bronte are *unequivocally on the side of the blues,* whereas the works of Alexander Pope, John Masefield, and Ezra Pound are not. Similarly, in painting, the blues could only wholeheartedly welcome and honor such figures as Bosch, Uccello and Van Gogh, just as it could only turn away from Rubens, Sir Joshua Reynolds and Rouault. Every form of human expression could be fruitfully reviewed through this infallible lens. As a poetic vehicle astonishingly free of the excess moral baggage of "civilization," the blues provides us with exemplary criteria, requiring total candor, a willingness to assume risks, an unfettered expression of the integral personality, an unreserved fidelity to one's deepest aspirations, an enthusiastic readiness for inspiration at all times. By the same token, the blues is absolutely incompatible with puritanism, Christian piety, dogmatism, smugness, Classicism, artifice, fascism, masochism — which, interestingly enough, happen to be the hallmarks of the dominant modes of poetry in English in this century.

The blues is thus a formidable breach in the wall that separates men and women from the revolutionary practice of poetry today. To prevent a possible misunderstanding, it should be noted that in the more than fifty years of its existence on records, and in the setting of the abominable social conditions with which it has had continually to contend, the blues could not possibly have remained consistently free of concessions. Indeed, many blues records, not to mention live performances, are repetitious, imitative and uninspired. But just as our view of Cubist painting is based on its best examples (the works of Picasso and Braque) rather than on minor and derivative works, so it is only to be expected that our conception of the blues as poetry should be based on the best, most imaginative, lyrics. Such lyrics, moreover, are sufficiently abundant to preclude the accusation that one must overturn a mountain of sand to retrieve a handful of pearls.

In all matters of evaluation one should heed Rosa Luxemburg's advice "to distinguish the essential from the non-essential, the kernel from the accidental excrescences." What is essential is this: not since the Elizabethan era, not even during Romanticism, has there been in English a sustained poetic *current* of such startling ingenuousness and purity, a poetic current so completely unencumbered by pretense and affection, a poetic current so imbued with the spirit of freedom and love, and so cognizant of the inseparability of the two.

Let us consider at this point the intellectual climate in which this revaluation is being made.

As the contemporary *crisis of consciousness* extends and gathers momentum, all existing institutions and values will be challenged and criticized without mercy. As our awareness grows of the real possibilities of the present and the future, our image of the past is also increasingly released from shackles of mystification. As the "History" sanctified by the fetishism of commodities loses its authority, the real history of men and women becomes a lever of human emancipation. And in the same way that the latent faculties of the mind increasingly flourish in such situations, permitting everyone to perform *miracles* unthinkable at other times, so many forgotten (i.e., suppressed) figures relegated to "long ago" are awakened from their enforced slumber and recognized as forerunners of the actualization of our own most ardent reveries.

The surrealists have already brought to light an extensive *accursed tradition* in U.S. culture — accursed in that it is ruled "out of order" by the existing authorities, largely neglected by scholars and critics, and not taught in the schools, as if such brutal evasions were sufficient to rub out the evidence. Today, here as everywhere, "the chickens are coming home to roost." Many heretofore "excluded" figures — mostly to be found in the academically unrespectable realm of "popular culture" — are receiving some serious attention at last and thus, are starting to be recognized as actively *subversive* influences.

Even a small sampling of the evidence suggests that the world will never be the same:

Comic artists such as Winsor McCay (creator of *Little Nemo in Slumberland* and *Dreams of a Rarebit Fiend*), George Herriman (*Krazy Kat*), and Carl Barks (*Uncle Scrooge*) are coming to be recognized as the bearers of more inspired revelations than most of the august acolytes of the Fine Arts. Animated cartoonists such as Tex Avery and Chuck Jones, creators of Bugs Bunny and the undisputed masters of the convulsive gag, have brought an unprecedented oneiricism and poetic *excess* into visual humor.

Fantasy writers such as H.P. Lovecraft, Clark Ashton Smith and Frank Belknap Long, usually in popular "pulp" magazines, have recorded the terrors and exhilarations of the awesome dawn of a transitional epoch, exactly as did their precursors, the Gothic novelists, during the French Revolution. Several imaginative nonconformist thinkers such as Benjamin Paul Blood (author of *The Anaesthetic Revelation* and *Pluriverse*), Ethan Allen Hitchcock (brilliant interpreter of alchemy), Paschal Beverly Randolph (author of *Magia Sexualis*), and Charles Fort (tireless chronicler of the unexpected) indicate an important underground current that upsets the cherished presumptions of what has passed for American Thought. A number of storytellers such as Charles Brockden Brown, Ambrose Bierce, O. Henry and Jack London, once popular but later suspiciously fallen to low critical esteem, also merit revaluation in the light of current poetic needs. Several writers heralded by the surrealists practically defy classification: T-Bone Slim wrote columns overflowing with plays on words and revealing a profound receptiveness to the "secrets" of language, published in the press of the Industrial Workers of the World (IWW), the revolutionary labor union. Samuel Greenberg, dead in 1917 at the age of 24, after a life of indescribable torment and poverty, left behind some of the most magical poetry in English, none of it published in his lifetime.

Several self-taught architects, such as Simon Rodia (who built the resplendent towers in Watts, California, scene of the great black insurrection in 1965), and S. P. Dinsmoor (builder of the "Garden of Eden" in Lucas, Kansas), have exposed the manipulative emptiness and lack of heart characteristic of the loathsome official architectural regime. The great film comedians Buster Keaton, Harry Langdon, W. C. Fields and the Marx Brothers offer an unparalleled critique of everyday rationalism and mediocrity, hinting at the creative playfulness sought by all.

These are but a few of the heroic figures on the *other side* of the "American dream." It is no accident that they have begun to appear in their true light, receiving the sympathetic attention they long have deserved, only with the advent of surrealism in the U.S. For the same forces that recently have brought into being an indigenous surrealist movement in the U.S. have also enabled us to perceive clearly the significance of its various isolated antecedents.

Appreciation of this accursed tradition, of which surrealism is the most advanced and revolutionary expression, can only enhance the contemporary appreciation of the blues. For the blues singers belong to the same heroic company. Their work, like that of the others we have named, is emblazoned with all the colors of the future. Held in check by the repressive forces of the past, they are reborn today in the fever of our wildest dreams. They are all anticipations of *that which will be.*

It goes without saying that jazz also belongs in this context, and a few words on the relationship of blues to jazz would be appropriate. If the blues singer is "naive," the contemporary jazz musician most assuredly is not. But it is noteworthy that the central figures at each turning point in the development of jazz have derived much of their *force of propulsion* precisely from a return to the blues. Compared to the primitive vitality, energetic self-confidence and lusty exuberance of early Storyville jazz and blues, swing — in its best-known and most commercially successful (i.e., white) forms — could be viewed as a kind of "counter-revolution." But bebop represented a "negation of the negation" and consequently a new affirmation, a vehement *rallying to principles:* indeed, its impassioned return to the roots is inseparable from its advance.

The Bebop Revolution was followed in turn by "cool" or "progressive" jazz, an eminently respectable genre quickly subsumed into the white middle-class collegiate and advertising-executive milieu. But the new dialectical movement — represented chiefly by John Coltrane, Eric Dolphy and Ornette Coleman — went even deeper into the roots than had bebop. A Coleman composition such as *Ramblin,* as one writer has observed, seems "to reach back to some unnamable country music beyond the Robert Johnson of *Hellhound On My Trail* (McCarthy *et al.* 1968:50). Coleman was, in fact, a bluesman for years before achieving the *definitive transmutations* for which he is best known. Dolphy and Coltrane, too, were deeply imbued with the blues, as evidenced by the former's astonishing solos on "Charles Mingus Plays Charles Mingus" and by Coltrane's albums "Blue Train" and "Coltrane Plays the Blues."

More recent developments have taken a diffuse and even confused form: after the dull-witted eclecticism of the "Third Stream" and new commercial degradations like the "Bossa Nova," the jazz market (*sic!*) all but collapsed in consequence of the wholesale revival of Rock. The authentic poets of jazz necessarily entered a period of profound occultation. It is evident, however, that the proponents of the tendencies in jazz which are "absolutely modern" (in Rimbaud's phrase) — Albert Ayler, Cecil Taylor, Roscoe Mitchell, Pharaoh Sanders, Sun Ra,

McCoy Tyner, Richard Abrams, Joseph Jarman — operate under the magisterial sign of the primordial blues.

The fact that the spirit of the blues is preserved in the most audacious currents in jazz by no means implies that the blues itself is incapable of autonomous renewal. On the contrary, the blues is a kind of automatic phoenix, perennially reborn, an ever-recurring original source. The simultaneous appearance in black music of Charles Mingus and a "naive" J. B. Hutto is no more surprising than the simultaneous appearance in painting of Wifredo Lam and a "naive" Hector Hyppolite. The blues seems anachronistic only to those who are unaware that the Golden Age lies not in the past but in the future.

J. B. Lenoir remarked that "nobody can sing the blues if he has never been blued; nothing can come out of you unless it's in you" (Broven 1964). Thus a bluesman has crystallized into a powerful maxim the honor and pride and vigilance of the blues. The magnificently undiplomatic straightforwardness of this "devil's music," as it has long been called, and its sensitiveness to the cries from the farthest reaches of consciousness, make its message all the more urgent in the face of the organized incoherence and hypocritical malevolence of the existing social order.

We are living at a time when it is possible for a best-selling book to bear the contemptible title *Beyond Freedom and Dignity* in which its author, B. F. Skinner, proposes a system of "behavior modifications" which calls to mind only the billy-club and the concentration camp. Now, if blues and jazz stand for anything, they stand for freedom and dignity. We could paraphrase Marx and say that blues and jazz are revolutionary or they are nothing. Those who are charged with preserving existing social relations at all costs are trying desperately to make them nothing — by promoting the impoverished and debilitating effusions of Rock and at the same time more or less deliberately *suppressing* authentic blues and jazz, by cutting off their possibilities for extension and proliferation in their natural milieu.[2] The very isolation imposed today on blues and jazz people alike is, itself, a proof not only of the continuity of their irreducible radical essence but also of the fact that the "Establishment" feels threatened. The specter of Afro-American music continues to haunt the white power structure.

It is Leon Trotsky who wrote that "the dialectic of the historical process has more than once cruelly punished those who tried to jeer at it." Whether its chosen instrument happens to be Memphis Minnie's National guitar or Ornette Coleman's white plastic alto saxophone, the dialectic is also preparing the victory of blues and jazz over those whose jeers never have been anything more than the rattling chains of the old order.

The "devil's music" — that is, the music of the damned, the music of the excluded — embraces the revolutionary principle of *evil* which Hegel long ago recognized as the form in which the motive force of historical development presents itself. Through its "deliberately obscure language of concealment" (Oliver 1968:11) one finds in the blues old but neglected truths gushing forth in geysers of inspiration prophesying the eventual triumph of the damned over those who now hold the reins of power; as an oft-quoted lyric announces, "The sun's gonna shine in my back door some day." Blues and jazz have their place among the chosen vehicles by which paradise will be established on Earth.

Miraculously *incorrigible* in every sense, the blues has remained one of the most precious subterranean reservoirs of authentic poetry throughout this century. For the development of this unique gift, far from the universities and garrets where the official "poets" devised their lamentable priesthoods, we should all be profoundly grateful. The time has come to render homage to those black working men and women of remarkable genius and lucidity who, in the destitute farmlands of the South and later in the ghettoes of the North, gave us works in which poetry retains all its limitless grandeur and always reaches out for more.

November 1973

Notes

1 See his collection *Rana Mozelle* in the Surrealist Research & Development Monograph Series (Chicago: Black Swan Press, 1972), as well as other writings in *Arsenal/Surrealist Subversion* and other collective publications.

2 It is too little known that many outstanding blues singers, such as Johnny Shines and J. B. Hutto, have long been unable to find more than sporadic employment. The modern revolutionary jazz musician fares no better. The great pianist Cecil Taylor, who has worked as a dishwasher in clubs that featured his records on the jukeboxes, argues that this enforced isolation from the "public" is an intentional bourgeois maneuvre to fragment all opposition.

BIBLIOGRAPHY

ARAGON, Louis. "Le Surréalisme et le devenir révolutionnaire." *Le Surréalisme au service de la révolution* 3 (Paris, December 1931) 2-8.

Arsenal: Surrealist Subversion 1, Chicago, 1970.

Arsenal: Surrealist Subversion 2, Chicago, 1973.

BLAKE, William. "The Marriage of Heaven and Hell." *Complete Writings,* Oxford University Press, London, 1966.

BLOOD, Benjamin Paul. *The Anaesthetic Revelation and the Gist of Philosophy.* The author, Amsterdam, NY, 1874.

BRETON, André. 1924 "Introduction to the Discourse on the Paucity of Reality." *What is Surrealism? Selected Writings of André Breton,* ed. Franklin Rosemont (Monad Press, New York, 1978).

1928a "Surrealism and Painting." *Surrealism and Painting* (Harper & Row, New York, 1972; Macdonald & Co, London, 1972) 1-48.

1928b *Nadja.* Grove Press, New York, 1960.

1937 *De l'humour noir.* Editions G.L.M., Paris, 1937.

1940 *Anthologie de l'humour noir.* Editions du Sagittaire, Paris, 1940. [Reprinted with a new preface by the author, J.J. Pauvert, Paris, 1966.] *Anthology of Black Humor.* City Lights, San Francisco, 1997.

1944 *"Silence is Golden." What is Surrealism? Selected Writings of André Breton* [see above.]

1947 "Hector Hyppolite." *Surrealism and Painting* [see above] 308-12.

1952 *Entretiens.* Gallimard, Paris, 1952.

1956 "Aloys Zötl." *Surrealism and Painting* [see above] 354-5.

1969 *Manifestoes of Surrealism.* University of Michigan Press, Ann Arbor, MI, 1969.

1972 *Surrealism and Painting.* Harper & Row, New York, 1972; Macdonald & Co, London, 1972.

BROVEN, John. "J.B. Lenoir." *Blues Unlimited* 15 (September 1964).

CALAS, Nicolas. "The Meaning of Surrealism: an Interview." *New Directions 1940* (New Directions, Norfolk CT, 1940) 385-95.

CÉSAIRE, Aimé. 1939 *Return to my Native Land.* [New ed., with preface by André Breton.] Présence Africaine, Paris, 1971.

Discourse on Colonialism. Monthly Review Press, New York, 1972.

CHARTERS, Samuel B. *The Poetry of the Blues.* Oak Publications, New York, 1963.

CREVEL, RENÉ. *Le Clavecin de Diderot.* Editions Surréaliste, Paris, 1932.

DARAUL, Arkon. *Witches and Sorcerers.* Wehman Brothers, Hackensack NJ, 1962.

DEREN, M. 1952 *Divine Horseman: Voodoo Gods of Haiti.* Dell Publishing Co, New York, 1972.

DEVEREUX, G. 1959 "Art and Mythology: a General Theory." *Art and Aesthetics in Primitive Societies,* ed. C. Jopling (E.P. Dutton & Co, New York, 1971), 193-224.

DUNNE, J.W. *An Experiment with Time.* Faber & Faber, London, 1958.

ESMAN, A.H. "Jazz: a Study in Cultural Conflict." *American Imago* VIII (1951), 219-26.

EVANS, David. *Tommy Johnson.* Studio Vista, London, 1971.

FAHEY, John. *Charley Patton.* Studio Vista, London, 1970.

FAIRBAIRN, W.R.D. "Prolegomena to a Psychology of Art." *British Journal of Psychology* 28 (1938), 288-303.

FENICHEL, O. *The Psychoanalytic Theory of the Neurosis.* W.W. Norton Co, New York, 1945.

FERENCZI, Sandor. 1913a "Stages in the Development of the Sense of Reality." *Sex in Psychoanalysis* (Basic Books, Inc, New York, 1950) 213-39.

 1913b "The Ontogenesis of Symbols." *Sex in Psychoanalysis* [see above] 276-81.

 1914 "The Ontogenesis of the Interest in Money." *Sex in Psychoanalysis* [see above] 319-31.

FINKELSTEIN, Sidney. *Jazz: a People's Music.* The Citadel Press, New York, 1948.

FINN, Julio. *The Bluesman.* Quartet Books, London, 1986.

FRAZER, J.G. 1911 *The Magic Art. (The Golden Bough* I & II.) The Macmillan Co, New York, 1966.

 1913 *The Scape Goat. (The Golden Bough* IX.) The Macmillan Co, New York, 1966.

FREUD, Sigmund. 1900 *The Interpretation of Dreams. (Standard Edition* IV & V.) Hogarth Press, London, 1953.

 1901 *The Psychopathology of Everyday Life. (Standard Edition* VI.) Hogarth Press, London, 1960.

 1905 *Jokes and Their Relation to the Unconscious. (Standard Edition* VIII.) Hogarth Press, London, 1960.

 1908 "Character and Anal Eroticism." *Standard Edition* IX (Hogarth Press, London, 1959), 169-75.

 1918 "From the History of an Infantile Neurosis." *Standard Edition* XVII (Hogarth Press, London, 1955), 7-122.

1927a "Humor." *Standard Edition* XXI (Hogarth Press, London, 1961), 161-6.

1927b *The Future of an Illusion. Standard Edition* XXI (Hogarth Press, London, 1961), 5-56.

FROIS-WITTMAN, J. "Preliminary Psychoanalytic Considerations of Modern Art." *Archives of Psychoanalysis* I, (1927) 891-941.

GARCIA-LORCA, Federico Francisco. 1930 *Poet in New York.* Grove Press, New York, 1955.

GARON, Paul. 1970a "Blues and the Poetry of Revolt." *Arsenal: Surrealist Subversion* 1 (1970) 24-30.

1970b "If The Blues Was Reefers. . . ." *Living Blues* 3 (Autumn 1970) 13-8.

The Devil's Son-in-Law: The Story of Peetie Wheatstraw and his Songs. Studio Vista, London, 1971.

"The Dirty Dozen." *Living Blues* 97 (May/June 1991)

"White Blues." *Race Traitor* 4 (Winter 1995) 57-66. Reprinted in Noel Ignatiev and John Garvey, eds. *Race Traitor.* Routledge, New York, 1996, 167-175.

GENGENBACH, E. "Lettre à André Breton." *La Révolution Surréaliste* 8 (Paris, December 1, 1926) 29-30.

GOJA, H. 1920 "The Alteration of Folk Songs by Frequent Singing: a Contribution to the Psychology of Folk Poetry." *The Psychoanalytic Study of Society* III, ed. W. Muensterberger & S. Axelrad (International Universities Press, New York, 1964), 111-70.

GRUVER, Rod. 1970 "The Blues as Secular Religion." *Down Beat Music Annual '70* (Maher Publications, Chicago, 1970) 24-9.

GURALNICK, Peter. *Feel Like Going Home.* Outerbridge & Dienstfrey, New York, 1971.

HARRIS, Wilson. *Tradition, the Writer and Society.* [With an appendix by C.L.R. James.] New Beacon Publications, London & Port of Spain, 1967.

Heatwave 2, London, 1966.

HEGEL, G.W.F. 1835 *On Tragedy.* Ed. A. & H. Paolucci. Doubleday & Co, New York, 1962.

HOFFMAN, Lawrence. "Guest Editorial: At The Crossroads." *Guitar Player* (August 1990)

JABLONSKI, Joseph. "Blues, Dream and the Millennial Visiion." *Living Blues* 25 (Jan-Feb 1976) 32-33

JONES, Ernest. 1919 "The Theory of Symbolism." *Papers on Psychoanalysis* [Fifth Edition] (Beacon Press, Boston, 1961), 87-144.

On the Nightmare. Hogarth Press, London, 1931

JOSEPHSON, M. *Life Among the Surrealists.* Holt, Rinehart & Winston, New York, 1962.

KARDINER, A., and Ovesey, L. *The Mark of Oppression.* World Publishing Co, Cleveland OH, 1962.

KEIL, Charles. *Urban Blues.* University of Chicago Press, Chicago, 1962.

KOHUT, Heinz. "The Psychological Functions of Music." *Journal of the American Psychoanalytic Association* III (July 1957) 389-407.

KOVEL, Joel. *White Racism: a Psychohistory.* Random House, New York, 1970.

KRIS, Ernst. *Psychoanalytic Explorations in Art.* International Universities Press, New York, 1952.

LEIRIS, Michel. 1946 *Manhood.* Grossman Publishers, New York, 1963; Jonathan Cape & Co, London, 1963.

"On the Use of Catholic Religious Prints by Practitioners of Voodoo in Haiti." *Evergreen Review* 13 (1960) 84-94.

LEONARD, Neil. *Jazz and the White Americans.* University of Chicago Press, Chicago, 1962.

MABILLE, Pierre. *Le Miroir du merveilleux.* [With a preface by André Breton.] Les Editions de Minuit, Paris, 1962.

MADDOX, Conroy. "Notes on the Christian Myth." *Free Unions Libres* (London, 1946) 14-5.

MAGLOIRE-SAINT-AUDE, C. *Dialogue de mes lampes, suivi de Tabou et de Dechu.* Premiére Personne, Paris, 1970.

MARCUSE, Herbert. *Eros and Civilisation.* Beacon Press, Boston, 1955. *Five Lectures.* Beacon Press, Boston, 1970.

MARGOLIS, N. "A Theory on the Psychology of Jazz." *American Imago* XI (1954), 263-91.

MARX, Karl. 1844 *Economic and Philosophic Manuscripts of 1844.* International Publishers, New York, 1964; Lawrence & Wishart, London, 1970.

MCCARTHY, Albert, et al. [eds.] *Jazz on Record: 1917-1967.* Hanover Books, London, 1968.

MEISSNER, W. "Notes on Identification. III. The Concept of Identification." *Psychoanalytic Quarterly* XLI (1972) 224-60.

MÉNIL, R. "Generaltés sur "l'écrivain" de couleur antillais." *Légitime Défense* (Paris, 1932) 7-9.

METRAUX, A. *Voodoo in Haiti.* Schocken Books, New York, 1972.

Minutes. 1909 *Minutes of the Vienna Psychoanalytic Society,* ed. H. Nunberg

& E. Federn. Volume II (1908-10), Session 66, 117-24; Session 73, 179-84. (International Universities Press, New York, 1967.)

MOON, Bucklin. "Louis and the Blues." *Record Changer* (September 1953) 9.

NEWTON, Francis. *The Jazz Scene*. MacGibbon & Kee, London, 1959.

NOUGE, Paul. 1929 "Le Conference de Charleroi." Published in English translation as *Music is Dangerous* (Surrealist Research & Development Monograph Series), Black Swan Press, Chicago, 1972.

ODUM, Howard W., and Johnson, Guy B. *Negro Workaday Songs*. University of North Carolina Press, Chapel Hill, 1926.

OLIVER, Paul. *Blues Fell This Morning*. Cassell & Co Ltd, London, 1960; Collier Books, New York, 1963 [retitled *The Meaning of the Blues*]. *Conversation with the Blues*. Cassell & Co Ltd, London, 1965; Horizon Press, New York, 1965.
   Screening the Blues. Cassell & Co Ltd, London, 1968; Oak Publications, New York, 1970 [retitled *Aspects of the Blues Tradition*].

O'NEAL, Amy. 1971-2 "Koko Taylor." *Living Blues* 7 (Winter 1971-72) 11-3.

OSTER, Harry. *Living Country Blues*. Folklore Associates, Detroit, 1969.

OTTENHEIMER, Harriet. 1973. *Emotional Release in Blues Singing: A Case Study*. Tulane University PhD Dissertation, 1973.

PAALEN, W. 1944 "On the Meaning of Cubism Today." *Form and Sense* (Wittenborn & Co, New York, 1945), 23-30.

PÉRET, Benjamin. "Magic: the Flesh and Blood of Poetry." *View* 111:2 (1943) 44-6, 63, 66.

PREBLE, E., and Casey, J., Jr. "Taking Care of Business: the Heroin User's Life on the Street." *The International Journal of the Addictions* IV (1969), 1-24.

PUCKETT, Newbell Niles. *Folk Beliefs of the Southern Negro*. University of North Carolina Press, Chapel Hill, 1926.

RADCLIFFE, Charles. "The Blues in Archway Road." *Anarchy* 5 (Freedom Press, London, 1965) 129-33. [Published under the pseudonym "Ben Covington."]

RATCLIFF, A.J.J. *A History of Dreams*. Small, Maynard & Co, Boston, 1923.

Resurgence 8, Chicago, 1966.

RICKLIN, F. *Wishfulfillment and Symbolism in Fairy Tales*. Nervous and Mental Disease Publishing Co, New York, 1915.

RIGAUD, M. 1970 *Secrets of Voodoo*. Pocket Books, New York, 1971.

RIGAUT, J. c. 1927 "New York." *Ecrits*. Gallimard, Paris, 1970.

RISTIC, M. "L'Humour, attitude morale." *Le Surréalisme au service de la révolution* 6 (Paris, 1933) 36-9.

RODGERS, T. "The Evolution of an Active Negro Racist." *The Psychoanalytic Study of Society* I, ed. W. Muensterberger & S. Axelrad (International Universities Press, New York, 1960), 237-47.

RODNEY, W. *The Groundings with My Brothers*. [With an introduction by Richard Small.] Bogle-L'Ouverture Publications, London, 1969.

ROEDIGER, David R. *The Wages of Whiteness*. Verso Books, London and New York, 1991.

ROEDIGER, David R. *Towards the Abolition of Whiteness*. Verso Books, London and New York, 1994.

RÓHEIM, Géza. *Animism, Magic, and the Divine King*. Alfred A. Knopf, New York, 1930.

> *The Origin and Function of Culture*. Nervous and Mental Disease Publishing Co, New York, 1943.

> *The Eternal Ones of the Dream*. International Universities Press, New York, 1945.

> *Psychoanalysis and Anthropology*. International Universities Press, New York. 1950.

ROSEMONT, Franklin. "Preliminary Reconnaissance of Surrealist Cultural Revolution." *Surrealist Insurrection* 3 (Chicago, August 1968).

> "A Revolutionary Poetic Tradition." *Living Blues* 25 (Jan-Feb 1976) 20-23

> "Black Music, By Any Means Necessary." *Living Blues* 25 (Jan-Feb 1976) 23

> "Black Music and the Surrealist Revolution." *Arsenal: Surrealist Subversion* 3 (1976) 17-27

> ed. *Surrealism and Its Popular Accomplices*. San Francisco: City Lights, 1980.

RUBINFINE, D. "Notes on a Theory of Depression." *Psychoanalytic Quarterly* VII:3 (July 1968) 400-17.

SCHAFER, R. *Aspects of Internalization*. International Universities Press, New York, 1968.

SILBERER, H. *Problems of Mysticism and its Symbolism*. Moffat, Yard & Co, New York, 1917.

SLONIMSKY, N. "Surrealism and Music." *Artforum* V (September 1966) 78-85.

SOURIS, A. 1966 "Paul Nougé et ses complices." *La Surréalisme,* ed. F.
Alquié (Mouton et Cie, Paris, 1968), 432-54.

STERBA, R. "Some Psychological Factors in Negro Race Hatred and
in Anti-Negro Riots." *Psychoanalysis and the Social Sciences* I, ed.
Géza Róheim (International Universities Press, New York, 1947),
411-27.

SUMMERS, Montague. 1927 *The History of Witchcraft and Demonology.*
[Reprinted by University Books, New York, 1956.]

SZEKELEY, L. "The Creative Pause." *International Journal of Psycho-
Analysis* XLVIII:3 (1967) 353-67.

TALLANT, R. *Voodoo in New Orleans.* The Macmillan Co, New York,
1946.

TEIGE, Karel. "Photo, Cinema, Film." *Change* 10 (Paris, 1922) 55-77.
[In French, translated from Czech.]

TEODORESCU, V. 1970 "Leninism and the Structure of the Poetic
Image." *Arsenal: Surrealist Subversion* 2 (1973) 33-4.

THIRION, A. 1972 *Révolutionnaires sans révolution.* Editions Robert
Laffont, Paris, 1972. [Translated into English by Joachim
Neugroschel as *Revolutonaries without Revolution.* NY: Macmillan,
1975.]

WINNICOTT, D.W. *Playing and Reality.* Basic Books Inc, New York,
1971.

INDEX

Name occurrences in the Afterword
and footnotes are not indexed.